OKANAGAN COLLEGE LIBRARY

P

01488709

Offering Sm

D0843982

E 98 .T6 P36 1988
Offering smoke : the sacred
Paper, Jordan

148870

DATE DUE

JUN 29 1994	
NOV 22 1994	
DEC 07 1994	
FEB 22 1995	
MAR 08 1995	
NOV 29 1999	

BRODART, INC.   Cat. No. 23-221

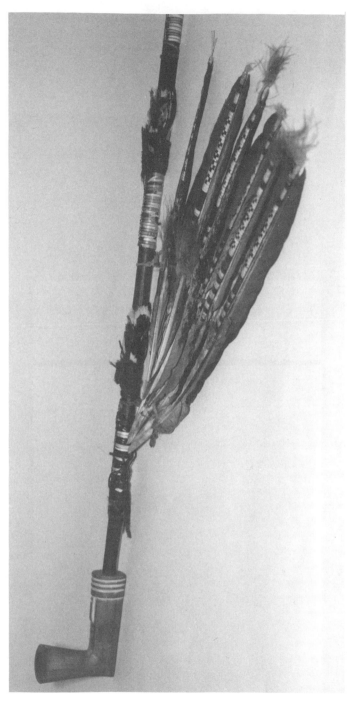

1. *Ojibwa pipe collected ca. 1830. The stem is typical for pre-eighteenth-century decorated stems.*

OKANAGAN UNIVERSITY COLLEGE
LIBRARY
BRITISH COLUMBIA

Offering Smoke

*The
Sacred Pipe
and
Native American Religion*

Jordan Paper

THE UNIVERSITY OF IDAHO PRESS
MOSCOW, IDAHO

Published by the University of Idaho Press
Moscow, Idaho 83843

©1988 by Jordan Paper
Designed by Caroline Jean Hagen
All rights reserved.
Printed in the United States of America
96 95 94 93 92 91   5 4 3

Library of Congress Cataloging-in-Publication Data
Paper, Jordan.
    Offering Smoke.

    Bibliography: p.
    Includes index.
    1. Indians of North America—Tobacco-pipes.
2. Indians of North America—Religion and mythology.
3. Indians of North America—Rites and ceremonies.
I. Title.
E98.T6P36 1988   299'.74   88-28378
ISBN 0-89301-126-6 (pbk.)

THIS BOOK IS DEDICATED TO THE BIDASSIGEWAK NATIVE WAY
School community, with gratitude, and to the memory of R. Clark
Mallam, who, by his life, exemplified for me the terms: husband,
father, scholar and friend.

Contents

List of Illustrations

Maps and Table

Preface

THIS WORK BEGAN AS AN INTERDISCIPLINARY STUDY OF THE
Sacred Pipe, combining methodologies from archaeology, art history,
cultural anthropology, ethnohistory, ethnology, and history of religions.
Because the Sacred Pipe is the core ritual and symbolic heart of many
Native traditions of North America, the research led to an analysis of
major aspects of Native American religion as a whole and to revisions of
established anthropological theories. The evidence indicates that contemporary pipe-centered pan-Indian religion is a revitalization of a major
religious modality that has as long a history as virtually any other in the
world. The research also led to a reassessment of the role of women and
of female spirits in Native American religion, a role found to equal
that of the male.

This book has come from a journey that began sixteen years ago.
Along the way many people and institutions aided me; this work is
more theirs than mine. It is not possible to mention by name all those
who have helped, and I apologize to the many not listed.

This work is about that which is central to Native American spirituality, and it could and would not have developed had it not been for
the many Native people who helped me gain a degree of understanding. John-Paul and Marilyn Johnson first showed me the reality behind
the books. Joe Couture pointed the way. Jim Dumont and Edna
Manitowabi and the community in which they live opened their hearts
and homes to me and enabled me to learn directly from the source of
understanding. Pauline Harper and Vern Harper shared their lives with

me. The children of the Wandering Spirit Survival School taught me how to communicate. Art Solomon gave me a task. Although everything I have learned is due to these generous people and others, what is expressed in this book is my responsibility alone. Not all, I think, will agree with every point I have made in the following chapters. I trust they will accept that I must be true to the understanding I have been given.

(The names for the Native peoples used in this book are not, in most cases, those used by those peoples for themselves. To avoid confusion and use of bracketed names, the names given are those in the books cited and in the museums surveyed. Often these are the names used by a people's enemies. For this I apologize.)

Many of my academic colleagues have helped me in this work. Among them, Chris Vecsey of Colgate University, Amanda Porterfield and Dan Merkur of Syracuse University, and Ted Brasser of the Canadian National Museums have been particularly supportive in facilitating this study. Ake Hultkrantz provided the methodological stimulus which his pioneering works on pan-Indian religious ideology (1953, 1957). John Berthrong of the United Church of Canada enabled me to participate in events that proved to be important to this book.

During my travels, a number of scholars shared their insights with me. I would particularly like to thank Ed Newberry, D.C. Cole, John C. Ewers, and Robert Hall. The research could not have taken place without the assistance of the following museums and their staff members, who generously gave their time, in a period of staff reductions, to facilitate my work with the collections: (in order of research) Museum of the American Indian, Department of Anthropology of the Smithsonian Institution, Anibal Rodriguez of the American Museum of Natural History, Diane Fane of the Brooklyn Museum of Art, Ron Weber of the Field Museum of Natural History, Milwaukee Public Museum, Dan McPile of the Thomas Gilcrease Institute, National Museum of Man, Liza Churchill of the Glenbow-Alberta Institute, Patricia McCormack of the Provincial Museum of Alberta, Royal Ontario Museum, Staffan Brunius of the Etnografiska Museet, Dr. Andreas Lüderwaldt of the Übersee Museeum, Dr. Axel Schulze- Thulin of the Linden-Museum, Kathleen Skelly of the Peabody Museum of Archaeology and Ethnology, and a number of smaller local museums.

This work could not have been accomplished without the generous assistance of the Social Science and Humanities Research Council of Canada, which supported for two years the extensive travel and photographic expenses required by the research. My own Faculty of Arts at York University awarded me a fellowship, freeing me of all teaching and administrative duties for a year to write the manuscript, and supported some of the publication expenses; I would not have managed the time to write it otherwise.

I am grateful for the considerable patience shown by my wife Chuang Li and my children, Eli and Leila, in tolerating my many disappearances over a period of years to participate in ceremonies, to travel many times for museum and library research, and to become oblivious of all but a computer screen as I wrote the manuscript.

Finally, I would like to express my gratitude to Those who guided this work and enabled it to come to fruition.

Meegwetch.

Acknowledgments

THE AUTHOR WISHES TO EXPRESS APPRECIATION TO THE FOLLOWING museums for permission to publish his own photographs from their collections:

AMERICAN MUSEUM OF NATURAL HISTORY: catalogue numbers 50/598, 50/5413, 50.1/5853, 50.1/8421A, 50.1/9849, and 50.1/9850.

BROOKLYN MUSEUM OF ART: catalogue number 06.64a.

FIELD MUSEUM OF NATURAL HISTORY: catalogue numbers 14901, 44066, 51632, 61457, 66601, 69554, 71718, 71872, 96821.

LINDEN-MUSEUM: catalogue number 40283.

MUSEUM OF THE AMERICAN INDIAN: catalogue numbers 2/4419, 2/7133, 2/8363, 10/4494, 12/3093, 21/545.

MILWAUKEE PUBLIC MUSEUM: catalogue numbers 2761, 4447, 13978, 14027, 14022, 14023, 14095, 14101, 14250, 20222, 31492.

NATIONAL MUSEUMS OF CANADA, NATIONAL MUSEUM OF MAN: catalogue numbers III-G-310, III-G-311, III-G-825, III-G-826ab, III-G-1098, V-E-300.

PROVINCIAL MUSEUM OF ALBERTA: catalogue number H80.5.4ab.

SMITHSONIAN INSTITUTION, DEPARTMENT OF ANTHROPOLOGY: catalogue numbers 90306, 90307, 395329.

ÜBERSEE MUSEUM: catalogue number C8225.

Osage Ritual Song

The Holy pipe
Holy, I say
Now it appears before you
The Holy pipe, behold you.

[The Sacred Pipe] is the most mysterious
thing in the World. The Scepters of our
Kings are not as much respected; for the
Savages (sic) have such a Deference for
this Pipe, that one may call it the God
of Peace and War, and the Arbiter of
Life and Death.

Father Marquette, 1673

PROLOGUE

Pipe and Tobacco in
Native American Religions

A MODERN PIPE CEREMONY

IN A MIDWESTERN INNER-CITY PROTESTANT CHURCH SHOWING ITS age, a gathering slowly grows in the large social hall. It is an evening in the mid-1970s. The people include Ojibwa, Odawa, Mohawk, Cree, Micmac, métis, and a few non-Natives. Among the latter are the minister of the church, a Catholic priest, a psychiatrist who has Native patients, and a university professor whose courses touch on Native religion. The gathering is under the auspices of a Native women's group that has use of the church's facilities.

As people enter, they gather in small groups, quietly talking, anticipating the special event of the evening. Once the quiet is disturbed by a drunk who has to be ejected from the hall, but the patient, waiting mood quickly returns. The group grows large, to almost a hundred. Many have never been to the women's group's evenings before; word had spread far concerning this particular evening's activity.

Eventually the crowd's attention is caught by a small group entering the hall. Deference is shown to the awaited person and his helpers, who live over half a day's drive away. After those known to the person are individually greeted, the gathering is asked to sit or kneel on the floor in a circle, which becomes a large oval because of the numbers and the shape of the room. Women sit on the north side of the circle and men on the south side. Menstruating women are asked to sit just outside of the circle. Those who have drunk alcohol within the past four days are asked not to directly take part.

As the leader and his helpers sit at the western extreme of the circle, a quiet excitement can be felt among the people. One helper passes the smoke from a burning braid of sweetgrass over each person in the circle. Another helper removes a plain wooden stem, a simple stone pipe bowl, a pouch of tobacco, and a tamper from a leather bag. A hush falls over the group; the hall is empty of sound but filled with presence.

While the leader explains the impending ritual to the people present, the helper incenses the pipe with sweetgrass and joins the two parts together. He fills the pipe pinch by pinch, each purified with the smoke of sweetgrass and prayed over. The leader sings a sacred song, lights the pipe, and offers the smoke to the spiritual powers by pointing the stem towards the four directions, towards the sky, and towards the earth. A helper takes the pipe and begins to bring it to each person in the circle in a clockwise direction.

The few who have participated before in pipe rituals take the pipe and perform brief rituals with it. They motion the pipe upward and touch it to the floor before smoking or turn the pipe in a circle afterward. Some wave the smoke from the pipe over their heads, and some state "all my relations" as they pass the pipe to the person on their left. For most, the pipe is brought to their mouths by the helper and they place their hands on the stem. The stem is touched to the foreheads of infants too young to smoke.

As the pipe slowly moves around the circle, those to whom the pipe has not yet come wait in calm anticipation, those who have smoked are left in still reverie. By the time the pipe has gone halfway around the circle, the tobacco in the bowl has all turned to ash. Yet the pipe is still passed from lips to lips, hands to hands, to complete the circle. When it returns to the leader, another song is sung, and the pipe is reverently taken apart. The ceremony is over.

All who have participated are profoundly moved. Most have never previously had the opportunity to participate in a pipe ceremony, although they had long been aware of its importance. Some have tears in their eyes; many feel transformed. There is a feeling of a new era—the Sacred Pipe has returned to the people.

What is this plain ceremony that brings many different people to join together in a common experience of the numinous? What is this unadorned ritual object that elicits such awe? What is this simple act that has the potential to transform a person's life? What is this brief event that leads Native people to regain surety in their own culture and themselves? It is to these questions that this book is addressed.

TOBACCO IN NATIVE AMERICAN RELIGIONS

If there is one aspect unique to aboriginal religion in the Americas, it is the ritual use of tobacco. As noted by an eighteenth-century observer: "All the Indian nations we have any acquaintance with, frequently use it on the most religious occasions" (Adair 1775:408). Elsewhere in the world one can find such relatively common particulars of Native American religion as the ritual use of sweat ceremonials, fermented beverages, dog sacrifice, and shamanic trance. The focus on tobacco as the primary sacred plant is ubiquitous throughout the Americas save for the Arctic, but in parts of Central and South America other sacred plants may be of equal importance.

The word "tobacco" apparently was based on a linguistic misunderstanding by Columbus and the early Spanish who applied a Carib word for a Y-shaped inhaling instrument to the plant itself. The early French explorers utilized their version, "petun," of a Brazilian Tupi word for the plant, even in northern North America (West 1934:31-33).

Tobacco is classified botanically as the genus *Nicotiana* Linnaeus, named after a sixteenth-century French ambassador to Lisbon, Jean Nicot. It belongs to the nightshade family (*Solanaceae*), which includes the potato and eggplant. Of the at least sixty-four species in the genus, most are native to the Americas (Wilbert 1986:1). Wild species in Australia are not used for smoking, but the aboriginal people there do chew the leaves (Watson 1983).

Although it is questionable whether tobacco is technically a hallucinogenic substance (Schultes 1972:53-54), it is used in healing practices among Native peoples in Central and South America in ways similar to the use of psychoactive plants (Wilbert 1972). Nicotine liberates the neurotransmitter norepinephrine, which is chemically related to the hallucinogenic mescaline, and releases the hormones epinephrine, dopomine and serotonin. The latter is related to two hallucinogenics, psilocybin and psilocine (Wilbert 1986:147-148).

Wilbert (1986:149-200) documents examples of "tobacco shamans," who use tobacco to induce trance, in tropical South America. In these circumstances, massive amounts of tropically grown tobacco are rapidly smoked and otherwise ingested, along with other psychoactive plants. The cigars used can be over eighteen percent nicotine (Siegel et *al*:22).

The same tobacco, *N. rustica* L., grown in northern North America is in certain respects a different plant. Due to the considerably shorter growing season and cooler climate, the leaves are much smaller and contain less nicotine. The amount smoked is considerably less than in Central and South America. Although nicotine creates a physiological and psychological state of well-being and is addictive, tobacco seems not to be ritually used to induce trance outside of the tropics and subtropics in both North and South America.

Modern domestic tobacco is derived from *N. tabacum* L. of Caribbean origin, which has supplanted the original domesticant in eastern North America, *N. rustica* L., grown extensively throughout the eastern half of North America. The precontact range of *N. rustica* L. in North America approximates the range of the sacred pipe before the adoption of the horse and westward spread of the fur trade, as will be discussed later. In the Plains, three other varieties were grown, and several further varieties were grown on the west coast of North America (Haberman 1984).

N. rustica L. is an attractive plant that varies in height from two to four feet, depending on climate and soil, and has medium-sized leaves and small yellow blossoms. Both dried leaves and blossoms were smoked. The leaves dry green, the preferred color, in shade. The plant is rather hardy, although sensitive to the contemporary acid rain, and is self-seeding.

In discussing tobacco in Native religion, one is discussing not only varieties of the genus *Nicotiana*, but other substances either mixed with *Nicotiana* or smoked in its place. In North America, these alternatives are, most commonly, the inner bark of certain trees of the genus *Cornus*, such as red osier, the leaves of one of the sumacs (*Rhus glabra*) when they have turned red in the autumn, and the leaves of bearberry (*Arctostaphylos uvaursi*). All these plants have an association with red, a color representing blood, the essence of life—the outer bark of red osier is as named, red; sumac leaves turn brilliant red; bearberry has red berries, and the dried leaves are similar to the green of Native dried tobacco leaves. The Algonkian word, "kinnikinnick," is variously applied to a smoking mixture as well as to individual elements.

Although tobacco is chewed, snuffed, particularly in the Amazon region, and drunk as an infusion of the leaves, especially when mixed with more potent substances, as in the "black drink" of southeastern North American cultures, its most common use is to produce smoke through burning. In North America, the primary purpose of the tobacco smoke is as an offering to the spirits.

In offering tobacco to spirits, it is not necessary for the person making the offering to inhale the smoke. Tobacco is most commonly offered by being placed on coals or thrown on fire. Many cultures that smoke tobacco through pipes, cigars, or cigarettes of burning leaves, also offer tobacco directly on the fire. Tobacco need not even be burned, but may be placed on the ground as an offering to the earth, thrown on water, or placed on or by sacred rocks and trees. In the eighteenth century, the trader Long (1791:43) noted tobacco thrown on the water before his party proceeded onto Lake Superior. Whenever herbs, trees, animals, and stones are taken for use, especially sacred use, tobacco is placed by the requested substance as it is asked to offer itself to meet human needs.

Tobacco, offered directly or as smoke, allows for communication with the spirits. As a Mesquakie told a student seeking to understand Native American culture: "We use it [tobacco] in ceremonies; we throw it in the fire, and then we can talk to the spirits" (McTaggart 1984:120). The founder of modern anthropology, Lewis H. Morgan, noted that "The Iroquois believed that tobacco was given to them as the means of communication with the spiritual world" (1851:164).

In being thrown on fire or coals, tobacco in North America becomes similar to the sacred fumigants. These traditionally included cedar leaves in the east, sage and sweetgrass in the plains, and juniper and pine needles in the southeast. The smoke from the leaves or grass is used to purify the place, participants, paraphernalia, and offerings used in ceremonies. The desirability of tobacco as an offering to the spirits may have been discovered in the distant past in the ritual use of fumigants.

The parents of cultivated tobacco may be the oldest domesticant in the Americas, dating to over eight thousand years ago (Furst 1976). It is generally accepted among scholars that tobacco spread from South to North America, although it has been argued that the pipe spread in the reverse direction (Hall 1983:52). Such diffusion would have taken place at least several thousand years ago. The earliest evidence for horticulture in eastern North America, preserved squash seeds, dates to over three thousand years ago (Adovasio and Carlisle 1984), corresponding to the earliest tubular pipes, dated to between four thousand (Hall 1983:42; Penny 1985:26) and three thousand years ago (Brose 1985:53).

The growing of tobacco is generally quite distinct from the growing of plant foods. In some cultures, the Crows, for example, only tobacco is domesticated (Lowie 1919). Among the Narragansetts, Roger Williams (1634) observed: " . . . tobacco . . . is commonly the only plant which men labor in, the women managing all the rest" (McGuire 1899:417). Pierre Boucher (1664) noted a similar pattern among the Huron (Kinietz 1965:19). Iroquoian-speaking people only partially domesticate the plant, allowing it to self-seed, as among the Cayuga, or only broadcast the seed with no further cultivation, as among the Seneca (Linton 1924:3-4). In Mesquakie culture as in many others, only a few select people had the sacred duty and right to grow tobacco for the community as a whole (McTaggart 1984). In all cases, tobacco horticulture requires special rituals and is an especially sacred act.

These aspects of tobacco domestication indicate the religious significance of tobacco and suggest it may have been the first domesticant in North America. Although the earliest evidence for tobacco to date, carbonized seeds, is but two thousand years old (Haberman 1984), tobacco in North America is probably at least as old as the earliest horticulture. Tobacco seeds are extremely small and flotation techniques are both recent and time-consuming. Dottle analysis is unrewarding because it is still unclear how long nicotine survives before it dissipates. Earlier evidence for tobacco use undoubtedly will be forthcoming as archaeological techniques continue to improve.

One further question on the use of tobacco for which there are opposing answers is whether tobacco was smoked for non-sacred purposes in precontact culture. Roger Williams (1634) early observed: " . . . I never see any [Narrangansett] take [tobacco] so excessively as I have seen men in Europe" (McGuire 1899:417-18). However, Western observations tend to be ambiguous and contradictory on this point since most remarks are chance descriptions by Euro-Americans who often did not realize the significance of Native activities. For example, sweat ceremonials were mistakenly understood by non-Natives as exclusively a hygienic practice rather than primarily as a means for communication with spiritual entities. Hence, observation of Native smoking was also often interpreted from the European secular use of tobacco; secular because there was no cultural background for religious use. Furthermore, the distinction between secular and religious activity is rarely as clear-cut in non-Western cultures as it is in Christian culture. Nevertheless, following trade of tobacco by Euro-Americans to Native American peoples, primarily nonreligious use of tobacco certainly became common.

An appropriate comparison in this regard might be with the use of alcohol in other cultures. It is a general anthropological understanding that the use of fermented beverages began in human culture in a religious context. The distinctly different and ritualistic social behavior for drinking alcoholic beverages in modern Western culture is a vestigial reflection of earlier ritual use. In the development of Christianity, alcohol came to be used symbolically in the Eucharist. In Judaism and Chinese religion, as counterexamples, the actual drinking of wine remains a major feature of rituals. As a corollary, all drinking of wine in these two culture maintains strong ritual connotations; hence, in East Asia, alcohol is rarely drunk without food, maintaining the pattern of sacrificial meals.

Where the ritual connotations are maintained, as in Judaism and Chinese religion, alcohol abuse is uncommon, whereas it is common in Christian cultures. In those Native American cultures where ritual inebriation was an essential element of major ceremonies, from the Southwest southward, alcohol abuse seems to be less of a problem than in the northern Native American cultures, where the use of alcohol was introduced by Europeans. Never having been a part of ceremonial life, alcohol has no religious context and its imbibing has led to serious personal and social problems.

If this pattern of alcohol use is extended to tobacco use, an explanation of the latter appears. With the ready availability of different-looking commercial tobacco that was not ritually grown or prepared, Native people began to smoke tobacco outside of private or communal ceremonial contexts. Even today, in cultures as diverse as Mesquakie and Iroquoian, native tobacco, ritually grown, is reserved for ceremonial offerings. However, similarly to use of wine in Judaism and in China, "secular" use of tobacco maintains "sacred" overtones. Tobacco, even smoked outside of ceremonial contexts, never loses its special aura.

WAYS OF RITUALLY USING TOBACCO

The simplest means of offering tobacco to the spirits is to place the leaves directly in or on the earth, water, sacred stones and plants, and the remains of animals or spirits. Captain John Smith noted in 1607 that "these people have a great reverence for the sun above all things, at the rising and the setting of the same they make a round circle on the ground with dried tobacco, then they begin to pray." In 1608, he refers to the native people of Virginia throwing tobacco on rivers and the sea as an offering (McGuire 1899:548). Father Allouez, relating his experiences at Green Bay, Wisconsin in 1674, writes, "When they [the Illinois] pass the church, they throw tobacco all around it, as a token of respect 'to the greatest divinity of whom they have ever heard' " (West 1934:67). Of course, the Illinois may have so placed the tobacco to protect themselves from the missionary's foreign spirit.

Other nonsmoking uses of tobacco include snuffing the powdered leaves into the nasal passages, chewing the leaves, ingesting the powdered leaves mixed with other substances, using enemas, and imbibing liquid infusions from the leaves, often as a purifying emetic. Snuff was common to a number of areas of the Caribbean and South America. Often a forked pipette was used for inhaling the powdered leaves or drinking a liquid infusion. Chewing tobacco or placing powdered tobacco, usually mixed with lime, in the mouth, was practiced from California south through much of South America. The Jivaro of the northern Amazonian forest drink a tobacco infusion to regurgitate their guardian spirit for shamanic purposes (Harner 1973:20). Further examples of these usages will be found in Wilbert (1976).

The most common means of offering smoke to spirits is the most direct: throwing the leaves on fire or placing them on coals. Jean de Brebeuf (1636) noted that the Hurons threw tobacco on the fire before addressing spirits (Thwaites 1896-1901:X, 159). This method is ubiquitous throughout North America. Secondary methods involve those making the offering to bring the tobacco smoke into themselves and then blow it towards the spiritual recipient. The sharing of the smoke between the one making the offering and the spirit receiving it creates communion between the two. The sacred smoke may also be spread over oneself or over objects and persons as a blessing.

There are several methods of smoking, often indicating regional preferences. The simplest is to place one's head over burning leaves and inhale. Next in order of complexity is the cigar, a roll of leaves ignited at one end, while the smoke is drawn into the mouth through the other. This was the most common method of smoking in the Caribbean and surrounding areas, and cigars are still used in religious practices by the highland Maya (for illustrations, see Robicsek 1978:17-18). Next in complexity is the placing of shredded tobacco in a tubular, combustible container such as a reed or rolled cornhusk. This method of ritually smoking tobacco is found from the American Southwest through much of South America. Finally, there are manufactured smoking devices, that is, pipes, which are the most common means of containing tobacco for smoking in North America.

This difference between the predominant forms of smoking in North and South America was noticed by early European observers. André Thevet (1575) wrote: "This plant [tobacco] is much esteemed by them [natives of Canada] . . . placing it in a cornet; and lighting the other end they inhale its smoke . . . Differing from their use of this powder our natives of the Antarctic [Brazil] take *Petun* in a Palm-leaf" (Stabler 1986:47-48).

Basically, the smoking pipe is a non-combustible container that holds burning tobacco at one end and allows the smoke to be sucked through the other end. The most elementary pipe form is that of a tube. A more convenient modification is to bend the tube, forming a pipe bowl and stem; this allows gravity to keep the tobacco in place. A further modification is to separate the stem and the bowl; this allows the stem to be longer and the bowl and stem to be made of different substances. The longer stem facilitates communal smoking and, more important, allows the stem to be ritually offered with both hands to the spiritual recipients. For more than a millennium, the separate-stemmed pipe has been the major means of communal smoke offering over much of North America, and its use has become the paramount Native North American ritual (see Chapter 5 for history and distribution).

THE SACRED PIPE

The distinguishing characteristic of the Sacred Pipe is that the bowl is separable from the stem and the two parts are kept apart except during ritual use. That the pipe consists of two parts is itself of symbolic importance and signifies to many Native cultures a pipe of religious conse-

DRAWINGS

2. This is the oldest Sacred Pipe found in an ethnographic context. [#118; Chapter I, p.9].

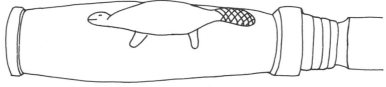

3. Piegan "Great Beaver Medicine Pipe." [#146; Chapter II, p. 25].

4. Pawnee ritual bundle pipe [#141; Chapter II, p. 32], similar in shape to Two Lance Bundle Society Bundle Pipe [#134].

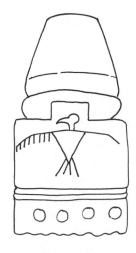

5. Blackfoot-type pipe with Thunderbird motif. [ROM HK930; Chapter III, p. 45].

6. Crow "Medicine Pipe" with lightning engraving. [#52; Chapter III, p. 49].

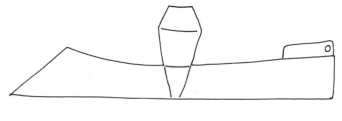

7. Sioux archaic style pipe [#182; Chapter III, p. 51], similar to Lakota tribal bundle pipe [#183].

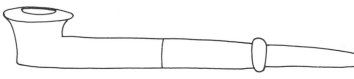

8. Hidatsa "flat pipe" used in eagle trapping ritual. [#64; Chapter III, p. 54].

quence. Two contemporary Native artists who create pipes as works of art write:

> Although the pipes we make for sale and display in museums and galleries are authentic and functionally smokable, "the stem is permanently attached to the bowl." In this way we make a personal statement to our people and to the public that our sacred objects are not for sale. To us a pipe whose stem is detachable from the bowl is a spiritual tool, beyond being an art object. (Freesoul and Freesoul 1984:8)

The bowl is usually made from stone and the stem most commonly from wood. Each part, as well as the joining of the two, is of considerable symbolic significance (see Chapter 4). The pipe itself is invariably considered holy and treated with veneration.

This pipe, prior to the contemporary spread throughout Native cultures in sub-Arctic North America, had a range from the Rocky Mountains to the Atlantic and from the Gulf of Mexico to James Bay. It did not penetrate to the Pacific coast where tubular pipes continued in use, nor among the cultures of the Southwest, where tubular pipes, termed "cloudblowers," and elbow pipes with a short reed stem continue in ritual use. In some cultures, the separate-stemmed pipe was and continues to be primarily used in a pan-Indian ritual context, as in the Iroquoian cultural complex, which had its own unique pipe form with a different ritual use.

The French, on first encountering the separate-stemmed pipe, called it a "calumet," from the medieval *chalemel* or *chalumeau* (reed) (see Springer 1981:230-31). This term has been since used with different meanings and has considerably confused discussion of the separate-stemmed pipe. Some scholars use the term only for an elaborately feathered stem, others for pipes used in a particular complex ritual, and yet others only for the particular ritual itself. Many scholars have applied the term to all separate-stemmed pipes but assumed the particular ritual complex was relevant to all such pipes.

Ignoring the original French use, but following convention, I will reserve the term *calumet* for the elaborately feathered stem used in rituals similar to the Pawnee Hako. Instead, for the sake of a convenient term, *I will call all separate-stemmed pipes "Sacred Pipes,"* including the calumet when the bowl is present. My distinction is similar to that of Hall (1983:51), except I include round- as well as flat-stemmed pipes.

Of course, all pipes used in Native ceremonials have a sacred function, but pipes such as cloudblowers and the Iroquoian type can be other-wise identified via existing terminology; except for the Pueblo cultures of the Southwest and tubular bone pipes in the Plains, only separate-stemmed pipes continue in religious use in North America.

It is generally accepted by scholars of Native American religions that the ritual of the Sacred Pipe, and the sweat lodge, are the most pervasive rituals throughout Native North America (e.g., Hultkrantz 1984). In a major bibliographic essay, Steinmetz (1984:27) emphasizes: "The Sacred Pipe in American Indian religions has a unique position in the history of primal religions throughout the world in the wide variety of symbolism associated with it and in its many ceremonial uses." Because of the sacred pipe's crucial role in virtually all rituals and its importance in origin myths, the Sacred Pipe is the key to understanding the origi-nal religions of North America from the Rockies to the Atlantic and from Hudson Bay to the Caribbean.

The centrality of the pipe to the religious life and understanding of many of the native peoples of North America can best be compared to the role of the Torah in Judaism and the Koran in Islam; it is the primary material means of communication between spiritual power and human beings. A 1939 address by an Assiniboine, Ochankugahe (Dan Kennedy), to students in Saskatoon exemplifies the Native American understanding of the Sacred Pipe (Petrone 1984:155-56):

> . . . let us explore that field seldom revealed to the whiteman — the inner sanctum of the Redman's soul. The most sacred of his rites is vested in the PIPE OF CHIEFS. To the Redman the Pipe of Chiefs symbolizes what the Magna Carta and the Ark of the Covenant stand for with other races. The Pipe is the medium and poetry of the Redman's plea to the Great Manitou. Over burning Sweet Grass the Pipe is incensed before it is proffered to the Manitou by the suppliant. As Moses of Biblical times received the Ten Commandments on the sacred tablets, so has the Redman the sacred Pipe as the symbol of the Manitou's Covenant. His moral, social and religious structure, his traditions, ceremonies and sacred rites are all deeply rooted in the ennobling influences of the Pipe. "Take this pipe," the Redman was commanded by the Great Manitou, "and with this Pipe you shall grow into nationhood. . . ."

From the standpoint of comparative religion, the Sacred Pipe is a sacrificial vessel. In many North American Native cultures, it is the primary means of offering the most sacred substance, tobacco smoke, to the sacred beings. Hence, it is comparable to the cast bronze sacrificial vessels of early Chinese civilization, the focus of that culture's creativity, technological development, and surplus economic productivity, to the degree that these vessels have since become the symbol of the civilization itself.

But the Sacred Pipe is not only a sacrificial vessel, it has a sacred nature of its own. Pipes that have been offered to the sacred powers may take on spiritual power themselves. Some pipes are considered so powerful that only individuals with shamanic power of their own can smoke them without being harmed. I have myself only literally experienced Kierkegaard's "fear and trembling" on approaching a particular pipe after experiencing firsthand the magnitude of power of that pipe and the spirit to which it was dedicated.

In the following chapters, the religion of the Sacred Pipe will be elucidated in four aspects: ritual, myth, description and symbolism, and geography and history. The two chapters on ritual and myth will discuss the religious nature and role of the pipe. Steinmetz (1984:27) has pointed out that "there has never been a comprehensive study of the Sacred Pipe in its religious significance." Although the material presented in these chapters is from published ethnohistorical data and ethnographic studies, this is the first attempt to integrate and analyze the scattered references from the methodological standpoint of history of religions. These chapters conclude with analyses of pan-Indian cosmology and theology in regard to the Sacred Pipe.

The research explicated in the chapter on description and symbolism is preceded by two voluminous studies, those of McGuire (1899) and West (1934). The former, although useful in its survey of early descriptive material, is unfortunately so imbued with the racism of its period that it is of little value, and it was written prior to scientific archaeology. The latter, written by a collector, is excellent in description but weak in analysis, particularly in regard to the religious significance of the pipe. The sections on symbolism will discuss the religious meaning of the pipe itself as well as its decor.

The first part of the chapter on geography and history is based on several years of ethnographic research in all of the major museum collections. It is intended to meet partially the suggestion of Springer (1981:230): "A thorough tabular survey of the elements of the smoking complex, including cartographic and statistical studies of the data, would allow us to ask more detailed questions." Such analysis leads to the conclusion that the Native American pipe ritual is a pan-Indian religious modality. Ethnohistorical research and studies of archaeological data adds the time dimension to this understanding. The conclusion is that this pan-Indian religious modality is of considerable antiquity, probably as old or older than the dominant religion of the invading Europeans. Throughout the four sections on the Sacred Pipe, it will be noted that the ritual role of women and the theological role of female spirits is considerably more important than the academic literature tends to imply.

Chapter 6, "Epilogue," will discuss the transition from the past to the present and survey the contemporary situation in regard to the Sacred Pipe. It is hoped that an understanding of the richness and antiquity of the pan-Indian religion of the Sacred Pipe will ameliorate the religious repression suffered by the Native American people of Canada and the United States. Those interested in further research will find a description of the methodology utilized in the first appendix and the essential data collected in the second. Most of the pipes discussed in the following chapters are detailed in this appendix, which is organized alphabetically according to culture of acquisition.

II

The Sacred Pipe in Ritual

NORMALLY IN STUDYING THE RELIGIOUS BEHAVIOR OF A CULTURE, one seeks ritual texts that determine if not describe the rituals. However, for nonliterate cultures, one must utilize less direct material. Sources generally are of two types. Ethnohistorical sources are pre-ethnological descriptions by foreigners. This type of data is usually partial and often contains misinterpretations, since the reporter naturally tends to interpret sense perceptions through the reporter's cultural filters. Ethnographic descriptions are written by ethnologists, trained in describing cultures other then their own. But early ethnolologists often focused on studying those aspects of culture important to their own culture rather than the culture studied, and, accordingly, were frequently oblivious to major aspects of ceremonial complexes, such as the sweat lodge and the important role of women. Native informants, too, had a tendency, in responding to questions, to attempt to provide the ethnologists with what they thought the ethnologist wanted to hear, rather than try to reinterpret the question so that it made sense within their own culture. Nevertheless, both types of accounts contain descriptions that when extracted and combined can create an understanding of rituals appropriate to the Sacred Pipe as well as its place in Native American religions.

This chapter on the ritual of the Sacred Pipe and its religious significance will be divided into four parts: ethnohistorical accounts, that is, descriptions from the sixteenth to the mid-nineteenth century; ethnographic descriptions, from the late nineteenth century to the present;

an analysis of pipe rituals in Native American religions; and the implications of Sacred Pipe ritual in delineating Native American cosmological and religious understanding.

ETHNOHISTORICAL DESCRIPTIONS OF SACRED PIPE RITUAL

Seventeenth Century

On landing near the mouth of the St. Lawrence in 1603, Champlain was welcomed with a pipe passed to him by people identified as Montagnais (Sauer 1980). Nearly a century earlier, in 1535, Cartier had noted pipe smoking along the St. Lawrence (McGuire 1899:419). Baird, in the same general area in 1616, noted: "All their talks, treaties, welcomes, and endearments are made under the fumes of this tobacco. They gather around the fire, chatting and passing the pipe from hand to hand" (Thwaites 1896–1901:III, 117).

Further south, as noted for Virginia in 1615, Europeans were also welcomed by being offered a pipe (McGuire 1899:377). Father Andrew D. White, in 1633, wrote of his experiences in Maryland:

> On an appointed day, there assembled around a great fire all the men and women from many parts of the country . . . some one produces a large bag; in the bag is a pipe and some powder which they call "potu." The pipe is such as our countrymen use for smoking, but much larger. Then the bag is carried around the fire . . . The circle being ended the pipe is taken from the pouch with the powder . . . and each one smoking it breathes over the several members of his body and consecrates them. (McGuire 1899:549)

The Spanish trader Diego Romero, who was ritually "adopted" by Plains Apache in present-day northeastern New Mexico or western Texas with a pipe ritual in 1660, observed the pipe, with a long wooden stem, held toward the sky and the earth (Kessell 1978:14). His father had participated in a similar ritual in 1634, and the other Spanish with Diego seemed familiar with it. (Because of his participation, Diego was charged with heresy by the Inquisition.)

In 1673, Father Marquette, seeking a route to China, reached the Mississippi River from the Wisconsin and began to travel down it (Lafitau 1724:II, 314):

It was the 25th of June the Indians, having recognized them as Europe-ans, sent four old men to speak with them. Two of them carried pipes to smoke tobacco in; they were highly ornamented and adorned with feath-ers of different sorts. They walked solemnly and raised their pipes toward the sun; they appeared to present it to him to smoke [i.e, stem first] without, however, saying a word . . . they were Illinois, and to guarantee peace they presented their pipes to smoke; then they invited him to enter their village . . . It is sufficient if one carries the calumet with him to show it, by which means they may walk in safety among enemies who, in the midst of fighting, will lower their arms to one who shows it. It was for this reason the Illinois gave this pipe as a safeguard among the nations through which they had to journey. There is a calumet for peace and one for war. They use them to end their differences, for strengthening their alliances, and to communicate with strangers.

It is made of a red stone polished like marble, and pierced so that one end serves to receive the tobacco, and the other has a socket for a handle, which is a stick two feet long . . . and pieced through in the middle. It is ornamented with the head and neck of different birds of the most beau-tiful plumage, to which they add also red, green, and other colored feathers. They regard it as coming from the sun, to whom it is offered to smoke when they want calm or rain or sunshine. (McGuire 1899:551–552)

Father Louis Hennepin (1698:125), in his travels in 1678, experi-enced similar pipes of peace, except he noted that the bowl can be of red, black or white "marble." He further noted that "They sheath that Reed into the Neck of . . . Huars [loons] . . . or else of Ducks who make their Nests upon Trees."

The above narrative of Lafitau continues by presenting the earliest detailed description of the "calumet dance" ritual (the first was recorded by Allouez for the Miami in 1667 [Thwaites 1896–1901:LI, 47–49]):

This calumet dance, which is very celebrated among these people, is not performed except on serious occasions . . . In winter the ceremony is held in a cabin; in summer out in the air. The place being selected they surround it with trees . . . There is spread out a large mat of reeds, painted different colors, in the middle of the place, which serves as a carpet for the god of him who makes the dance; for each one has his own, which is called his Manitou. It is a serpent, or a bird, or a stone, or some similar thing of which they have dreamed and in which they put every confidence for success in the war or chase. Sitting near this Manitou and on his right is placed the calumet in honor of the one who has given the feast . . . Things being thus arranged, those having the best voices, who are to sing take the most honorable places under the trees. All the world then comes and take their places around them, and as each one arrives he salutes the Manitou, which he does in smoking and blowing the smoke upon him, as though offering incense. Then the one who is to commence the dance appears and goes respectfully and takes the pipe and holding it in both hands he dances it in rhythm with the song. He makes it describe different figures; *at times he presents it to the company and turns it from side to side, then he offers it to the sun as though he wished him to smoke it; at others he inclines it toward the earth* [underlining mine]; sometimes he spreads his wings as though he wished to fly; at other times he places it in the mouths of the assistants that they may smoke it . . . it is like the first scene of the ballet. The second scene they imitate a combat . . . one with arms and another with the calumet. The third scene is a discourse, in which the one who holds the calumet tells of his victories and it is passed from hand to hand and they all have a chance to smoke.

La Salle (Margry 1875:553), in 1684, described a related ritual for the Arkansas, a difference being the use of two pipes. He also described the musical instruments used, being gourd rattles and what appear to be water drums.

Eighteenth Century

Du Pratz (1758:I,108) describes a similar pipe used in a peace ritual at the southern part of the Mississippi in 1719. Robert Rogers (1765:224), writing nearly a century after Marquette, describes a similar pipe as well as the differences between peace and war pipes, the latter being entirely red. This point was earlier noted by Charlevoix (1761:I,321) among the Onondagas in 1721. Jonathan Carver, in the northern Mississippi area in the 1760s, noted (1778:360) that the pipe was lit with a coal from the fire.

He then *turns the stem of it towards the heavens, after this towards the earth, and now holding it horizontally moves himself around until he has completed a circle* [italics added].

Each in turn who smokes "blows the smoke from his mouth first towards heaven, and then around him upon the ground."

Albert Pickett (1851:I, 130), quoting Charlevoix, who was among the Natchez at approximately the same time, writes of the grand chief at sunrise:

A pipe, which was never used but upon this occasion, was then handed to him, from which he puffed smoke, first toward the sun and then toward the other three quarters of the world.

William Bartram described a Creek council meeting of 1789. During the meeting he observed the pipe lit by the miko [chief], who then blew smoke first towards the east and then towards the other three cardinal directions; the pipe was then passed to the principal leaders and warriors and back to the *miko*, while all the others were taking black drink and smoking tobacco (Hudson 1976:229).

Early Nineteenth Century

Lewis and Clark (1814:I,364), noted the following details of the Sacred Pipe ritual when among the Teton in 1804:

They first pointed the pipe toward heaven and then to the four quarters of the globe, then to the earth, made a short speech, lighted the pipe, and presented it to us.

Stephen H. Long (1823:I, 208), who was among the Omaha a few years later, observed a pipe ritual prior to a bison hunt: The party having approached as near the herd as they suppose the animals will permit without taking alarm, they halt to give the pipe bearer an opportunity to perform the ceremony of smoking, which is considered necessary to their success. He lights his pipe and remains a short time with his head inclined. The stem of the pipe extends towards the herd. He then smokes and puffs the smoke towards the bison, towards the heavens, the earth, and finally to the cardinal points successively.

Prince Maximilian zu Wied (1839:I, 570), among the Crow in 1833, noted not only the smoke from the pipe blown toward the sun and then the earth, but that the pipe circulates sunwise:

. . . when the pipe circulates none take more than three [probably four] puffs, and then passes it in a certain manner to his left-hand neighbor (Davis and Ronnefeldt 1982:36).

George Catlin, among the Mandan at the same time, describing the major year-renewal ceremony, notes that the "medicine-man smokes his pipe in those [cardinal] directions" (Catlin 1844:I, 165).

The Swiss artist Rudolph Kurz journeyed through the Plains in 1851. He noted a Crow, on smoking the Sacred Pipe, lowering the bowl of the pipe to touch the ground (1937:262).

From the time of Marquette, Europeans were quick to learn to use the Sacred Pipe in their relations with Native Americans. Not accepting the sacred nature of the pipe themselves, Europeans abused Native respect for the Sacred Pipe for their own advantage in treaty-making and trade. Among many examples, at the beginning of the nineteenth century in the area of the Rocky Mountains, the trader Larocque gained advantage for himself with the pipe: "I told them many things which I thought was necessary and closed the Harangue by making them smoke the Medicine Pipe" (Burpee 1910:24).

Larocque closely observed rituals surrounding the pipe. He noted,

> The regulations common to all are these, the pipe and stem must be clean, a coal must be drawn out of the fire to light the pipe with, care must be taken not to light the pipe in the flames or ashes and none must empty the ashes out of the pipe but he that filled or lighted it (Burpee 1910:62–63).

A Native Account

All the above descriptions are by Europeans and Euro-Americans and reflect, at best, partial understanding. A virtually unique document is the recording of a Native American description for Native purposes. In the 1930s, Fred Gone recorded oral material by Garter Snake (1868–1953) from her father, Bull Lodge (ca. 1802–1886), keeper of the Feathered Pipe; this material was later edited by George Horse Capture. All are White Clay People ("Gros Ventre") of Montana. In this invaluable recording, there is a description of the pipe ritual Bull Lodge obtained from his visions and used in healing.

Garter Snake (1980:67) relates the first time her father was requested to heal. The requestor

> . . . filled a pipe with kinnickinnic and went to Bull Lodge's tipi. Standing where he entered, he asked Bull Lodge, 'How must I approach you with this pipe . . . "Come to me from your left," said Bull Lodge, "and

hold the pipe before you with stem foremost and with both your hands holding the pipe."

The requestor having done this,

> Bull Lodge took the filled pipe with both hands. Holding it in his left hand, he rubbed his right hand on the ground. He then stroked the whole pipe, starting at the far end and stroking towards his person. Then he changed the pipe to his right hand, and after rubbing his left hand on the ground, he stroked the pipe and stem towards himself. He performed this once more with each hand, so that the act was done four times.

Bull Lodge lit and smoked the pipe alternately with the person making the request. When the smoking was completed, the pipe was emptied with a fourfold ritual. The requestor was then handed the pipe and told to complete the circle of the tipi as he left.

The Iroquoian Pipe

The preceding descriptions of ritual are specific to the Sacred Pipe (separate-stemmed) and are to be distinguished from the ritual use of the Iroquoian pipe. This pipe, usually of clay, is of one piece with a short stem. Rather than being used for a communal offering of smoke to the spirits, it is smoked individually. In council, all seemed to smoke their pipes simultaneously. In an account of 1669, it was noted (Margry 1875a:128) that

> The Sonontonans [Senecas] to the number of fifty or sixty assembled in our cabins. Their custom is, on entering, to take the first vacant place, without regard to rank, and at once take fire for lighting their pipes, which are not taken from their mouths during the whole time of the council. They say that good thoughts come from smoking (McGuire 1899:550).

Such a council, perhaps of Huron, is illustrated on a 1657 map attributed to Bressani (Trigger 1985:102), where all the individuals in a council are shown smoking one-piece pipes.

The difference in use between the separate-stemmed and one-piece pipes was observed by Baron Lahontan (1703:I, 35). Among the

Onondaga in 1684, he noted that the chief sat in council "with his pipe in his mouth and the great calumet of peace before him."

ETHNOGRAPHIC DESCRIPTIONS

The last century has seen the publication of a voluminous literature on Native American culture of varying reliability. The centrality of the Sacred Pipe to religion is omnipresent. Peter Powell's (1969:I, 14) statement for one culture is, in general, true for all others east of the Rockies: "The Cheyennes say, 'The pipe never fails.' Nothing sacred begins without the offering of the pipe to the Sacred Persons who dwell at the four directions of the universe, to Maheo, and to Grandmother Earth." It is clear from the ethnohistorical data that Sacred Pipe ritual does not vary in its essential aspects from culture to culture. Therefore, the following presentation of ethnologically recorded pipe ritual is selective, based on the availability of relatively reliable and complete descriptions. (For a more complete list of accounts, see Steinmetz 1984.) For comparison, the ritual of non-separate- stemmed pipes is first presented.

Hopi

Pueblo culture maintains the ritual use of tubular pipes (Fig. 11) and also uses an elbow pipe with a short reed stem, and the separate-stemmed pipe has not been adopted. However, the ritual use of the pipe is similar to that of other cultures. J. W. Fewkes described the Hopi ritual pipe smoking to McGuire (570–571):

> The pipe bearer hands it [the pipe] to the chief, who smokes six whiffs to the north, west, south and east, then up and down on the altar. The chief then hands the pipe to the one on the left. The last man in the row hands it back to the pipe bearer . . . There is one head chief; the pipe bearer is next to the chief in dignity. The pipe used in the first eight songs of the sixteen-song dance is of the rectangular character [elbow with short stem] . . . after . . . the chief . . . puts the coal in a long, straight, conical [tubular] pipe holding six herbs . . . blows six puffs between the ears of a stone fetish [sic] of a mountain lion. No one else smokes this pipe.

Fewkes (1892:283) also noted: "They [Pueblo Natives] believe that the smoke is the cloud symbolized by it." Hence, the term, "cloudblowers," for these tubular pipes.

Blackfoot

One of the best ethnographic accounts of Native American religion was not written by an ethnologist. A member of a U. S. Forest Service expedition to northern Montana, Walter McClintock lived among the Algonkian-speaking Blackfoot from 1896 to 1900, having been adopted by Chief Mad Wolf, keeper of the important Beaver Medicine Bundle and a Sun Dance ritual leader. McClintock describes the adoption ritual (1910:26–35), including the use of the pipe. (In relating these rituals, McClintock clearly felt he was carrying out the purpose of his adopted father, Mad Wolf.) The ceremony is reproduced in some detail to provide an example of the context in which the Sacred Pipe is used.

. . . I found myself in a large, well ordered tipi of about twenty-five feet in diameter. Mad Wolf was seated at the back [facing east], the position of honour. His relatives were on either side, men to his left, and the women to the right . . . to [his] right . . . lay the sacred bundle of the Beaver Medicine. Next to it sat Mad Wolf's wife, Gives-to-the-Sun. . . .

All sat silently gazing into the small fire, for they were about to commence a religious ceremony . . . A large pipe of polished red stone was continually circulating, everyone smoking except the children. The pipe always started from Mad Wolf, who first blew four whiffs to the Sun and four to the Earth . . . Mad Wolf began the ceremonial by taking a hot coal from the fire with a long stick. He placed dried sweet grass upon it and the rising smoke soon filled the lodge with a pleasing fragrance. At this moment the clouds parted in the sky, and the sun came out. The bright rays, streaming down through the top of the lodge, shone upon the ground in front of Mad Wolf. Holding his hands in the sweet smoke of the incense, Mad Wolf passed them along his arms and upon his breast to purify himself, and then chanted:

"To-day, our father (Sun) shines into the lodge, his power is very strong.

"Last night our mother (Moon) shone into the lodge, her power is very strong.

"I pray the Morning Star (their Son) that, when he rises at daybreak, he too will shine in to bless us and to bring us long life."

Mad Wolf and Blessed Weasel together led a chorus in which all joined. The women held aloft their left hands and closely watched Mad Wolf, who with bent arms held his hands folded on a level with his head. Then passing his hands along his arms alternately, after their manner of a blessing, he finally folded them upon his breast, and chanted:

"Mother Earth have pity on us, and give us food to eat!

"Father, the Sun, bless all our children, and may our paths be straight!"

[After a ritual of blessing, the subsequent adoption rituals per se, and the singing of several songs accompanied by rattles,] Mad Wolf then danced around the fire with the pipe, singing and, at intervals, blowing upon his medicine whistle. Stock-stchi took the pipe from Mad Wolf. He blew four whiffs to the North, South, East and West, and then, holding the pipe towards the Sun, prayed to the Great Spirit in the Sun for the recovery of his sick child.

[Mad Wolf further prays to the Sun and the Moon, then] the wife of Blessed Weasel arose to ladle out the stew . . . When the stew had been passed to everyone . . . after a short pause, Mad Wolf said: "The berries that grow are blessed, for upon them we live." He held a sarvis berry in his right hand and chanted, everyone imitating his motions and joining with him in his prayer to Mother Earth that they might live to see many summers. After each person had planted a berry in the ground, a symbolic act in recognition of the source of their sustenance, they partook of the feast. None of the food was wasted. What remained was gathered together and set aside.

Approximately a week later, a Beaver Medicine ceremonial was held during which McClintock received a Blackfoot name. The Beaver Medicine bundle has associated with it a pipe given in mythic time by the Beaver Chief (1910:111). In the midst of the long, complex ceremony (1910:97–98):

It was now time to fill the sacred Pipe. Mad Wolf held the pipe bowl close to the tobacco. He slowly picked up the stone used as a stopper and placed it in the bowl [a straight pipe, see Chapter 4], leading a chant in which all joined: "The Sun beholds the smoke grow larger and larger." Picking up the pipe and tobacco he said, "The heavens provide us with seeds of the tobacco." Holding the tobacco up, he chanted, "I drop the seeds as I go along." He filled the pipe and prayed, "The place where I sit is sacred." Then holding up the pipe with the bowl pointed towards himself [and stem offered towards the spirit], he chanted:

Sacred Person! Behold I am still alive.
I ask the spirit of the wild geese to smoke with me,
The first that came into this country.
I know of no medicine as strong as my smoke.

> While going through the ceremonial with the pipe, the bowl became loose and fearing that it might fall, which would be an evil omen, Mad Wolf removed it.

(Robert Lowie noted [1935:270] a similar practice among the Crow: "A redstone bowl belonged with the outfit [Sacred Pipe bundle] but is taken off during the dance lest it drop.")

> He held up the stem and placing his right hand upon his breast gazed intently at the sun and chanted:
>> Sacred Spirit in the Sun, it has been a long time since you have smoked with me.
>
> He arose and danced, holding up the Sacred Pipe and blowing upon his medicine [eagle bone] whistle. Stock-stchi followed and the women also joined, all dancing in single file around the fire, following the direction of the sun's course through the heavens.

In other references to Sacred Pipe ritual, McClintock writes of women's pipes. For most cultures, female roles in ritual and specifically female rituals have not been recorded. The early ethnologists, either males or females trained by males, imputed Western patriarchal practices and values to Native people. Usually only a few weeks in the summer were spent with the observed group, with the ethnologist living in the nearest town with a hotel. Typically the ethnologist only discussed religious matters with males. Due to the writings of McClintock and others, we are more aware of women's rituals in Blackfoot and related (Blood and Piegan) cultures than for any other Native American culture.

Women's roles in Blackfoot rituals were crucial; they were central to the Okan (Sun Dance). Bundles, were, in effect, transferred to married couples, who were both responsible for their care (McClintock 1910:262–270; Wissler 1912; for a survey of the Plains medicine bundle complex, see Sidoff). Couples were jointly initiated into some secret societies, such as the Horns (see Wissler 1913).

In describing the transfer of a medicine pipe, McClintock (1910:266) describes an associated women's pipe that was only smoked by the women (for illustration, see Wissler 1913:415). During the Sun Dance ceremonial, McClintock (1910:295) mentions that at one point, "Two redstone pipes were passed around, one for the men and the other for the women."

At most other ceremonies, as mentioned above, the same pipe would be used by men and women.

The medicine pipes were band pipes; transfers remained within the band. In the spring, the bands came together for a joint pipe ceremony to greet the first thunder (Schaeffer n.d.). Concerning miscellaneous aspects of Sacred Pipe ritual, McClintock (1910:269) quotes the teaching that the medicine pipe keeper should not smoke with anyone who presses the tobacco into a bowl with the fingers rather than a tamper. This custom has also been noted for other cultures. G. A. Dorsey recorded that in ceremonial smoking among the Pawnee, the tobacco in the pipe must not be pressed with the finger, for the spirits to which the pipe is offered might assume that the smoker was offering him- or herself (Linton 1923:3).

Menomini

One of the earliest ethnologists, Walter J. Hoffman, obtained considerable data on another Algonkian speaking culture, the Menomini of Wisconsin in the 1880s. He presents a general but detailed account of the smoking of the Sacred Pipe (1896:251):

> When several Menomini are sitting together for social purposes, smoking is individual, and no offer of a pipe by one to another is made, unless the other desires a whiff, or may perhaps be without his own pipe. When sitting in council and having in hand the consideration of tribal affairs or deliberations relative to important social secrets, or when participating in ritualistic ceremonials, the smoker who fills the pipe hands it to his right-hand neighbor to light. The latter individual takes a few whiffs at intervals, inhaling each mouthful, after which the pipe is passed back to the owner at the left, who then takes several whiffs, when he passes it to the next person to his left. In this manner the pipe continues on its way around the circle, always to the left, until the bowl of tobacco is exhausted. He who concludes the smoking knocks out the ashes and hands the pipe to its owner.
>
> During the passage of the pipe silence is maintained, and if any conversation becomes necessary, it is conducted only in a whisper.
>
> At various intervals of ceremonial smokes, especially during the smoking preliminary to prayers and chants, puffs of smoke are directed toward the four cardinal points as well as toward the abode of the wind gods, or

the zenith — the abode of Kisha' Ma'nido — and towards the earth, the abode of the material parts of their deceased friends and relations. [Hoffman's last interpretation is suspect.]

The true Indian pipestem usually terminates in a cylindrical mouthpiece an inch or more in length and from one-fourth to one-third of an inch in diameter. When smoking, an Indian does not put this part into his mouth . . . but he will press it between the lips, and as the stem enters the mouth the outer and dry portion of the lips follow, so that the stem does not become moist. In sucking the stem and gaining a mouthful of smoke, the lips are slightly parted at either side or towards the corner of the mouth and air inhaled so as to mix with and pass down the throat into and filling the lungs.

Plains Cree

Alanson Skinner has recorded (1914:541–542) the pipe ritual of a bear feast for another Algonkian speaking culture, the Cree — here the Plains Cree of Saskatchewan. Bear is the most powerful of the earth spirits for many native people, and, although all hunted animals are accorded rituals, those for Bear are particularly significant.

On the evening of June 16, 1913, Neil Sauwustim shot a bear. The following day at noon the writer visited [Four-clouds's] camp where Sauwustim was staying and there partook of the Bear feast. The skin has already been removed and was lying folded up, head outermost [marked with yellow ochre and given a gift of red cloth], in the place of honor. [After the meat was cooked and distributed], Four-clouds filled the pipe, gave it to Spotted-one, and lighted it while he puffed. Spotted-one, then, as master of ceremonies, for he is a distinguished old man, smoked a few puffs and then offered the mouthpiece skyward praying that the day should be propitious and that no one should be injured while the sun shone. He then offered it to the ground with a prayer that the powers of darkness should be equally kind to men, then to the four world quarters with prayers to the winds, and last of all to the bear, telling it that it had been slain to furnish food, and begging its good will and future abundance of bears. He then passed back the pipe which was relighted and passed to the rest. Next Spotted-one raised the dish of bear meat before him above his bowed head as an offering to Gitce Manitou to whom he prayed. Lowering the dish he cut off some tiny morsels of each kind of flesh thereon, and cast them in the fire as a sacrifice.

Winnebago

Paul Radin studied the Winnebago, a Siouan speaking people contiguous to the Menomini, in the early twentieth century. He was particularly interested in religion and was among the Winnebago at a time when many were converting to John Rave's version, the most Christian, of peyote religion (see Chapter 6). On converting, they were exhorted to give up their traditional practices. Some did so by passing the rituals verbatim in Winnebago to Radin.

Among the rituals recorded are those connected with funerals (Radin 1923:92–107); the four-day major ritual begins with a ceremonial feast for the departed. Tobacco and water are given to the person who is asked to speak to the departed. After the speech of acceptance, he says:

> Here it is, the tobacco. I am certain that you, O ghost, are not very far away, that in fact you are standing right in back of me, waiting for me to reach you the pipe and tobacco, that you might take it along with you, that like-wise, you are waiting for your food to take on your journey. However, four nights you have to remain here.
>
> Now here are these things, and in return we ask you to act as mediator (between the spirits and us). You have made us long for you, and therefore do you see to it that all those things that belonged to you and that you would have enjoyed had you lived longer — such as victories on the warpath, earthly possessions, and life — that all these you leave behind for us to enjoy. This do you ask for us as you travel along. This also I ask of you, do not cause us to follow you soon; do not cause your brothers any fear. I have now lit the pipe for you.

The pipe is lit and passed around the participants. The speaker drinks from the bowl of water, which is then passed around as the pipe was. Then the food is passed and eaten (after, one assumes, a small portion of the food was offered to the departed). On the fourth night, the spirit is addressed and instructions are given on the journey to join the previously departed relatives, particularly on offering the pipe to spirits met on the journey to benefit the living.

Radin also provides bilingual verbatim accounts of the pipe ritual for clan war-bundle feasts (1923:420–423). In this ritual, the pipe from the bundle is filled four times, each time placed in the appropriate direction of the offering, while a sequence of the war bundle's songs are sung.

Lakota

James Walker was the agency physician at the Pine Ridge Reservation in South Dakota at the turn of the century. For nearly twenty years he questioned the elders and spokespersons about the religion and other aspects of Siouan speaking Lakota culture. From George Sword, we have an account of the pipe given in 1896 (Walker 1980:75–76, 82):

> When a Lakota does anything in a formal manner he should first smoke the pipe. This is because the spirit in the pipe smoke is pleasing to *Wakan Tanka* and to all spirits. If one is to smoke for another ceremony . . . he should sing a song or pray to a God while preparing the smoking material. Then he should take the pipe in his left hand, holding the bowl so that the stem does not point away from himself, and fill the bowl slowly.

(He later added [Walker 1980:82]: "The filling of the pipe is an important part of the ceremony. One may pray or sing while filling it.")

> . . . the pipe should be lighted with a coal of fire and not with a blaze . . . if more than one is to smoke they do so because the spirit in the pipe will make their spirits all agree. Then when the pipe is lighted it must be passed from one to another each smoking only a few whiffs, until the contents are consumed, and then the pipe should be emptied on the fire. If there is no fire burning, the contents should be emptied on the ground and carefully covered with earth . . . The smoke of the pipe may be made an offering by pointing the stem of a lighted pipe toward the one to whom the smoke is offered . . . There is a pipe that belongs to all the Lakotas. This is held by a keeper and kept from view except on important occasions when it is unwrapped with much ceremony and is only lighted when there are matters of interest to all Lakotas. When it is smoked, what is then done is binding on all the Lakotas.

Another account of the Sacred Pipe in Walkers's notes comes from Thomas Tyron (Walker 1980:148):

> The pipe is very *wakan* [sacred]. It is used for doing all things. It is used in all *wakan* actions . . . when they first light the pipe, they raise it up to the above and they say this, "Behold Wakan Tanka, I give this to you." They say, "I will live long and I will have horses; also, I will kill an

enemy." Or, "I will steal a woman," they say. They present the pipe to
the four winds and make these speeches.

And I will relate another different thing. If a man's child is sick, he
takes a pipe filled with tobacco to a [medicine] man . . . When going to
war or in the Sun Dance, the leaders carry the pipe.

Pawnee

Among Missouri basin and Plains native cultures, ritual warrior societies were a major feature of religious life. In 1902, James Murie observed
the Skidi Pawnee Two Lance Society's renewal of the lances ritual
(1914:561–567), which demonstrates the elaborate variations on basic
Sacred Pipe ritual that may develop. Only the society's members, excluding Murie, would have been present. Following the lance preparation
ritual per se, Known-the-leader announced, "It is now time to offer
smoke to the gods to show that we remember them . . . Knife Chief
will now rise and take the pipe I have filled."

> Knife-chief rose and took the pipe which belongs in a sacred bundle. It
> is very old; the bowl is large; the stem smooth and round and represents
> the windpipe through which the prayers of the people pass. Knife-chief
> walked around the fireplace with the pipe, beginning at the south. At
> the northeast he stopped and the south assistant lighted the pipe with a
> burning coal. He then walked around the fireplace by the west and then
> south with the lighted pipe and stopped successively at the south and
> north entrances and blew smoke in those directions. He next halted at
> the fireplace and blew smoke on its rim towards the northeast and the
> northwest. West of the fireplace he stopped and blew smoke southwest
> and southeast. Then he passed north and stopped at the west facing
> east. He blew smoke east, west, and then east again. Then he directed
> smoke towards the heavens; three times to the north, once to the south,
> faced about and blew smoke west. He turned again and blew towards the
> ground and the drums.
>
> The pipe was then passed to those on the north and the south sides,
> each person taking four whiffs. Knife-chief then strewed the ashes from
> the pipebowl west of the fireplace and facing west passed his hands over
> the pipe- stem, then over his own body, and handed the pipe to Known-
> the-leader who said, "Nawa." All the rest of the people said, "Nawa."
> This ended the first smoke ceremony.
>
> Known-the-leader again addressed the assemblage: "Men, old men
> and young men, another smoke offering is near. Our fathers [the lances]
> are completed and stand before us. We must offer them smoke. I have

filled this pipe. I have selected Brave-chief to carry on the smoke for he took part in war parties when these two lances were carried."

Brave-chief rose and took up the pipe. In the meantime, Known-the-leader's assistants took up the drums. At this point a song was sung about Father Owl, one about Father Crow, one about the Thunderbirds, while the last related to the lances.

Brave Chief walked around the fireplace, stopped at the west facing east, and pointed the pipestem upward. At the same time he took some tobacco from the bowl, raised it, gradually lowered his hand, and finally placed the tobacco in the rim of the fireplace. Then again he pointed the pipe to the rim of the fireplace and placed a pinch of tobacco on it. The first offering was in honor of Tirawahat, the second in honor of the earth. He sat at the northeast of the fireplace. Now the assistant on the north placed a coal on the bowl of the pipe and returned to his place.

Here followed, as at the first smoking, a complex ritual of smoke offerings.

Now food was placed east of the fireplace. There was one kettle of corn, a pot of meat, bread, and coffee. The corn was placed near the entrance. Known-the-leader said: "Old men and young men, the corn was given our women by Tirawa-hat. We were told to offer it to the gods. I select Knife-chief to make the offering, then we will partake of the food."

The corn was offered in a complex ritual similar to the first smoke offering. Afterwards the food was passed around.

Known-the-leader said: "Men, old men, young men, our fathers are now complete. Tomorrow we will have the dance. We have made the smoke offering to the gods and they will be thankful. We have also offered our corn to the gods and they will watch over us. We will now prepare to leave this tipi. We have eaten and smoked."

Murie notes that "the smoke and food offerings have practically the same form in all ceremonies."

Paviotso

For the last example of an ethnological report on a Sacred Pipe ritual, we return to the Southwest for the furthest westward extension of the separate-stemmed pipe. In 1933, Willard Z. Park observed curing ceremonies of the Paviotso in Nevada. The following description (1934:105) of ritual is limited to the use of the pipe; the full healing ritual is far more complex.

> Before dark the shaman comes with his kit, consisting of eagle feathers, eagle down, wild tobacco, stone pipe, and beads. He takes off his shoes and hat . . . He squats besides the sick person and smokes his pipe for a few minutes . . . He starts to sing . . . As soon as the people in the audience catch on to the song they help the shaman sing. Then he walks around the patient counter-clockwise.

Here follows repeated shamanistic sucking of the patient's illness, circumambulations, and songs.

> Finally, he stops, sits by the patient and lights his pipe. The pipe is passed around the fire counter-clockwise. Each person present takes one puff and passes it on to the next.

At this point the healer may go into trance. When he returns, he will explain the illness and spit out its cause.

ANALYSIS

As is normative for premodern human cultures, the Native American terms for one's own culture, in the many different languages, usually simply means "the people." The terms now generally used for most Native American peoples are the terms others, often enemies, used for them. Humans tend to only identify members of their own group as fully human. Others, not being fully or truly human, therefore, may be attacked and killed; hence, raiding and warfare are extensions of hunting.

Long-distance trade is evident from the material remains of Native American cultures over the last several thousand years. Copper from the western Great Lakes, red pipestone from the headwaters area of the Mississippi, and shells from both coasts and the Gulf of Mexico are found thousands of miles from their origins. Trade requires a way for strangers to become, at least temporarily, members of one's group. Hence, rituals of adoption become a necessity. Among many Native American cultures, an elaborate adoption ritual featuring a pipe with a feathered shaft became widespread, as seen, for example, in the Hako ritual of the Pawnee (see Fletcher 1904). The gift exchanges that were features of these adoption rituals were, in effect, the trade itself (see Will and Hyde 1917:171).

This ritual was found by Europeans in their earliest contacts with native peoples from the Mississippi to the eastern Plains as described in the preceding section. A number of scholars have confused the specific ritual complex of the "calumet" (see Chapter 1) with Sacred Pipe ritual in general. This in turn has led to incorrect theories of the spread of the sacred pipe. Fenton has understood Sacred Pipe ritual to spread with the French along the Mississippi and back to eastern North America. Turnbaugh (1977, 1979) has interpreted the ritual complex as a nativistic response to the crisis engendered by contact with Europeans. Hall (1977, 1983) has proposed an ingenious theory regarding the relationship of the feathered stems to atlatls and arrows. Springer (1981) has summarized the difficulties inherent in solely relying on written documents in developing theories of diffusion. Blakeslee (1987) has pointed to both ethnohistorical as well as archaeological evidence that the widespread ceremonial complex is older than contact with Europeans. However, he mistakenly focuses on a pipe shape that developed after the mid-eighteenth century (see Chapter 5) and finds the ritual complex spreading into eastern North America in the historic period.

All of these theories as well as others have reversed the development. The Sacred Pipe is not important because of the "calumet" ritual; rather, the Sacred Pipe is used in the "calumet" ritual because it is central to all rituals in North America. Crucial to the Sacred Pipe is its function as a means to offer smoke to sacred beings: all other functions are subsidiary. In some cultures, the feathered shaft of the "calumet" dance is not drilled through and is not a pipestem. In others, as described above, the bowl may be removed before dancing with the pipe, because the bowl is so revered, it must not be allowed to drop from the pipe. (Dancing is the most common method of praying and showing gratitude to the spirits in Native American cultures.)

Examining the actual preparation and smoking of the Sacred Pipe in a variety of rituals rather than focusing on only one ritual complex as a model will clarify the ritual use and religious significance of the pipe. As will be understood by anyone who has participated in North American native religions, the contemporary ritual described at the beginning of Chapter 1 is identical in all particulars with what is to be found in the ethnohistoric and ethnographic documents.

In using ethnohistorical and ethnological sources, I do not accept that view that if European or Euro-American observers did not notice or bother to record certain features, they did not exist. North American accounts are usually by the French or the English. Except for some early Spanish incidental accounts, such as Inquisition records, those of the early Spanish conquistadors, DeSoto for instance, were hostile and disdainful towards Native Americans and not likely to have been involved with ceremonials (cf. Swanton 1946:381). The further south and west the French and English travelled, the later their accounts. Little ethnology was done for native people east of the Mississippi, because many of those cultures had either been overwhelmed by Euro-American culture or forcibly removed to west of the Mississippi. If these anomalies in the ethnohistorical records are not taken into account, a skewed history is inevitable.

Basic to the ceremonial use of the Sacred Pipe is that it is passed among the participants: it creates social communion; it joins all into a sacred circle. Hence, Sacred Pipe ritual forms the basis of adoption rituals. This aspect of Sacred Pipe ritual is clear in all the early accounts: those of 1603 and 1616 at the mouth of the St. Lawrence River, 1615 for the mid-Atlantic coast, 1667 and 1673 for the upper Mississippi River, and 1684 for the lower Mississippi (Full references to these and the following accounts can be found on pages 18–35). This ritual feature is found at the western extreme of Sacred Pipe use in Nevada and is distinguishable from other ritual pipes such as the Iroquoian.

A major feature basic to Sacred Pipe ritual derives from the separate stem. The longer stem allows the mouthpiece of the pipe to be offered with both hands, a sign of respect around the world, to the spiritual recipients of the smoke offering. Universal to Sacred Pipe use is that the spiritual beings to whom the pipe and smoke are offered are either of the sky and the earth, or of sky, earth and the four directions (as well as the semi-cardinal directions for some cultures). These features can be found in the 1634 and 1660 accounts for the eastern part of the Southwest, 1673 and 1684 accounts for the upper Mississippi, late-eighteenth-century accounts for the lower Mississippi, 1804 account for the Rockies, and 1823 account for the middle Plains. These features are readily apparent in the ethnographic sources quoted.

Following the smoke offerings of the ritual leader, subsequent smokers as the pipe traveled about the circle offered puffs either to heaven and earth or four puffs to the spirits of the four directions or winds, as recorded for the upper Mississippi in the 1760s. Alternately, subsequent smokers may have motioned the pipe heavenward and touched the bowl to the ground, to indicate the offering to heaven and earth, as noted on the Plains in 1851.

The pipe usually circulated in the direction of the sun's travel, that is, to the left, as noted for the upper Missouri in 1833, and among the Menomini and Pawnee at the turn of the last century. However, a few cultures used a counter-sunwise direction, the Paviotso, for example.

Details such as lighting the pipe with a coal rather than fire were noted in the 1760s for the upper Mississippi and 1805 for the Rocky Mountains. In modern situations, especially in contemporary structures, that do not have a fire, matches or lighters may be used, but traditionalists often only light the pipe from a glowing braid of sweetgrass. That a tamper was used rather than fingers for symbolic reasons was noted for the Blackfoot and the Pawnee.

In making a request with the pipe, whether to spirits or a human person, one proceeds holding the pipe stem forward. This was noted in the mid-nineteenth century on the northern Plains.

The pipe not only allowed the smoke from the pipe, being breathed by both the spirits and the smoker, to create a communion between the offerer and the spiritual recipient, but the sacred smoke could be used as a blessing by motioning it over oneself. This was noted as early as 1633 in the Chesapeake Bay area.

The Sacred Pipe was used for all intertribal relationships, not only peace, but war as well. This was observed in 1673 for the upper Mississippi in 1719 for the lower Mississippi, and in 1721 for the Onondaga. This all-embracing use is also clear for late-nineteenth-century accounts of the Menomini and Lakota. In the 1870s, the Lakota brought a Sacred Pipe to the Navajo and Ute in New Mexico to request them to join in an uprising against the invading Euro-Americans. Although the Navajo decided not to join and were not a separate-stemmed-pipe-using culture, they kept the pipe. When a Lakota delegation again arrived in the 1890s, bringing the message of the Ghost Dance, the Navajo ceremonially greeted the Lakota with the pipe given them over a decade before (see Appendix II).

Finally, the use of the pipe by women has been obscured by ethnocentric Euro-Americans, in whose culture religious leaders in the past were almost invariably male. Father Steinmetz, a Jesuit priest, for example, cites this misunderstanding, that women do not smoke the pipe, as evidence for the "sacramental nature of the Sacred Pipe by way of contrast" (1984:30)! The Blackfoot pattern described above is not exceptional. Male ethnologists were invited to the ceremonials of male warrior societies; they would not have been invited to the ceremonies of female societies. Early female ethnologists often only considered males an appropriate source of religious knowledge. Hence, use of the Sacred Pipe by female religious leaders was either not noticed or ignored, or male use of the pipe was considered religious and female use social. In ceremonial gatherings that are not specific to either sex, men and women usually sit on opposite sides of the circle, but the Sacred Pipe is passed to all. (Menstruating women invariably do not take part in general Sacred Pipe rituals, because their innate power at this holy time will overwhelm the power of the pipe.)

COSMOLOGICAL IMPLICATIONS OF SACRED PIPE RITUAL

The cosmology of a culture is generally determined from the culture's religion, philosophy, or theoretical science. In seeking cosmology within religion, the tendency is to focus on myth. However, in regard to Native American religions, Hultkrantz (1979) has pointed out that myth and ritual are often separate, and that religion can best be understood through the latter. Western culture also intimately relates cosmology and cosmogony. This relationship assumes a linear concept of time with an emphasis on beginnings, which is itself particularly Western. In many North American Native cultures, except for the probable postcontact addition of Genesis parallels to migration myths (e.g., *Walum Olum* and Waters; see Paper 1983), the earth (not the cosmos as a whole) is created or recreated on the water, and these myths are often separate from cosmological understanding.

Native American rituals are based, in part, on an implicit as well as explicit cosmological understanding. An analysis of ritual movements within their symbolic contexts can lead to an understanding of this underlying cosmology. While most rituals are monocultural, there are major pan-Indian rituals that undoubtedly were extant before the arrival of Europeans. These rituals include sweat ceremonials, ubiquitous to most of the Americas, and the ritual of the Sacred Pipe, particular to North America.

Sacred Pipe ritual centers on the pipe itself; as the pipe is passed around the circle, so the center passes with it. The pipe is always at the center of the cosmos. The smoke is offered in all directions radiating outward from the pipe. This centering of the cosmos about the primary ritual feature at the time of the ritual is typical of Native American religions; e.g., the center pole of the thirst (or sun) dance, the fire of ritual lodges, and the pit in the sweat lodge and the kiva.

The bowl of the pipe is a sacrificial vessel that itself is a miniature cosmos. Often tobacco is added pinch by pinch, each explicitly dedicated to the sacred directions as well as animals and spirits, both therio and non-theriomorphic (as part of one's relations), thus bringing the entire cosmos into the bowl itself. The pipe stem, some older ones decorated with a striped design symbolic of the trachea, directs the offering towards the spirits. Eagle feathers may be hung from the stem to further symbolize the sending of the smoke and the accompanying vocal (or silent) petitions to the sacred persons. The primary smoker directs the smoke offering by pointing the stem towards the spiritual recipients, either before or after the pipe is lit. Subsequent smokers may offer the smoke with their mouth as well as by raising the pipe skyward, touching it to the ground, and turning the pipe in a circle.

The cosmos surrounding the pipe is spherical rather than circular or hemispheric. The offerings are directed towards the four cardinal directions (in a few cultures, the semi-cardinal directions), the zenith, and the nadir (the order varies). Euro-American observers often miss the totality of the directions because they do not observe the totality of the ritual movements, including the filling of the pipe. Subsequent smokers often indicate the zenith by motioning the pipe toward the sky, and the nadir, by touching the bowl of the pipe to the ground. The touching is appropriate because the bowl itself is understood as female, as is the earth (see Chapter 4).

In communal smoking, the ritual also indicates the cosmos of social relationships. At the center is the self, the one holding the pipe. Next comes the circles (in cultures with circular dwellings) of human relationships: family, clan, and "nation." Further outward is the sphere of animal relations: those who walk on the earth in the four directions, those who fly in the sky above, and those who crawl through the earth below or swim in the sea. Finally there is the sphere of the most powerful spirits: the Four Directions (Winds), the Sky and the Earth (Sea). Together these four spheres of beings form "all my relations."

Fundamental to cosmological understanding is the pairing of female and male spiritual powers that when combined, result in creation. The pipe itself consists of two parts, the bowl, which is symbolically female, and the stem, which is male. It is only when the stem is inserted in the bowl that the pipe is potent, and it is for this reason that the pipe is only joined at the beginning of the ceremony, and its separation indicates the termination of the ritual. Zenith and nadir, Sky and Earth, respectively are male and female; in their conjoining, plants and living creatures are created. So, too, the pipe bowl, with few exceptions, is of stone or clay, the substance of the female Earth, and the stem is usually of wood, from the procreated trees that rise toward the Sky.

However, the most common understanding of the zenith is more complex. For while the day Sky, the Sun, the West Wind, and the Thunder Beings are male, the night Sky, in particular the Moon, is female. So, too, while the Four Directions are Grandfathers, the South, the direction of growth and nurture, may be understood as female.

Once one goes beyond the basics of the directions, one is involved with monocultural understandings. Specific symbolic and mythic understanding of the meanings of the directions vary from culture to culture, even subculture to subculture. However, east and west are generally understood from the significance of the sun's path, symbolically equated with the path of life, as is the pipe stem itself. Accordingly, the ritual leader in a pipe ceremony normally faces east, the direction of the rising sun. The commonality of a fundamental cosmological understanding over most, if not all, of North America, despite major linguistic and cultural-ecological differences, helps explain why different Native American cultures could so readily borrow rituals from each other as well as maintain the common ritual of the Sacred Pipe.

Comparison with Sweat Lodge

Even more widespread than the ritual of the Sacred Pipe is the ritual frequently referred to in English as "sweat lodge." Although the ritual is usually part of all other major ceremonies, most ethnographic descriptions, where they mention sweat lodge at all, because of ethnocentrism misunderstand the ritual as a hygienic practice rather than a potent communal ritual of confession, catharsis, decision-making, and direct communication with sacred beings. The following description is a generalized summary from northern North American rituals, limited to those aspects relevant to the comparison. For modern descriptions, see Black Elk for the Lakota and Benton-Banai for the Ojibwa.

The sweat lodge is a dome-shaped structure, of which, as in any Native American ritual, every part has symbolic significance. The lodge is constructed from poles emphasizing the number four and its multiples, oriented toward the cardinal directions, with a low entrance usually facing east, the direction of the rising sun, symbolic of the beginning of life and understanding. In the center, a round pit is dug, the earth of which is used to form an altar east of the sweat lodge. Between the altar and the lodge is the fire, symbolic of the sun, which heats the stones used in the sweat ritual. When in use, the lodge is completely covered so it is light-tight.

The participants sit on evergreen branches or sage laid on the earth. If there are a number of participants, four are delegated as gatekeepers of the four directions, although there is but one physical opening, itself covered during the ritual. The pit is understood as the womb of the earth in which are placed the Grandfathers, the red-hot rocks that on taking on the energy of the fire, represent the sun as well as all other Grandfathers. (As substances of the earth, stones and rocks are female; it is the heat of the fire, symbolic of the sun, captured in the rocks that is male.) The Grandfathers are sprayed with water, the life-fluid of the Earth. From these actions comes regeneration. At the conclusion of the complex ritual, the participants crawl from the dark womb through the narrow opening, cramped, hot, wet, yet inspired. Born anew, they great each other and those outside anew as reborn persons.

Hence, the symbolism and ritual of the sweat lodge indicates the same cosmology as the ritual of the Sacred Pipe: the cosmos of the four directions, male zenith and female nadir, the latter two representing the creative forces of the cosmos. The commonality of the cosmological understanding of the sweat lodge with the ritual of the Sacred Pipe further points towards this understanding as fundamental to Native American cultures.

The cosmological understanding of female-male, earth-sky complementary polarity is so fundamental to Native American cultures that it is at times reflected in social divisions. For example, the Osage clans are divided into two moieties: Ho^n-ga, representing earth, land and water, and Tsi'zhu, representing sky (La Fleshe, n.d.).

III

The Sacred Pipe and Myth

BECAUSE THE DOMINANT WESTERN RELIGION, CHRISTIANITY, focuses on belief, that is, ideology, there is a tendency in religious studies to assume that the essence of a religion is expressed in its myth. Myth is the living expression of the fundamental understanding of a culture. In literary cultures, it is often assumed that since the myths are written they are fixed in time, but this is not the case. The Bible and the Koran are understood through theological interpretation that is constantly responding to changing cultural circumstances. In Buddhism, sutras were written for over a millennium and commentaries are still being produced.

On the other hand, ritual tends to be more conservative. The roots of the Eucharist are to be found in the Greek mystery religions and Mithraism. The primary ritual of Chinese religion has been little changed over at least four millennia (Paper 1988). As has been discussed in the previous chapter, the ritual of the Sacred Pipe has remained unchanged since it was first noticed by Europeans. However, several centuries of contact and eventual conquest by European Christianity has had its effects on Native American myths (see Hultkrantz 1980 and Paper 1983).

While ritual can be observed, even if not necessarily understood by outsiders, myth in nonliterary cultures is often inaccessible. The ritual of the Sacred Pipe is particularly available to outsiders, because it is a ritual of sharing, of communion; it is central to the rituals of adoption and friendship. Myths, on the contrary, are told in a ritual setting not necessarily open to outsiders. Alfred Kroeber (1907: 308– 309), in discussing the tribal symbol of the Arapaho, the "Flat Pipe" (see Chapter 4), writes that the tribal myth of the origin of the pipe is in the keeping of the guardian of the Flat Pipe and can only be told in a ceremony of four night's duration: "It has never yet been recorded by a white man even in fragments of any amount." Similarly, we are told that the old chiefs of the Osage considered the oral traditions of the tribal pipe "too sacred to talk about" (Fletcher and La Flesche:I, 188).

When such traditions have been recorded by ethnologists, care must be taken in the use of this information: the informant may have not been a person privy to the sacred teachings, the informant may have deliberately misled the ethnologist, the translator may have reinterpreted the material to please the ethnologist, or the ethnologist may have abbreviated the material according to her or his own values. Except under conditions of severe cultural change, the sacred myths are only imparted in a ritual context, and only by those who have the religious prerogative to do so. For example, I cannot recount those myths I myself have heard within a ritual context, because I do not have that right.

Nevertheless, a few accounts of myths concerning the Sacred Pipe, rarely complete, have been recorded. In this chapter, two types of these myths will be discussed: myths about how a particular Sacred Pipe was received, and cosmogonic myths in which the Sacred Pipe plays a major role. A third section concerns a myth about a stone often used for for the making of pipes. The final section will be an analysis of the Sacred Pipe in myth and religion and will present a theology of the Native religious traditions in which the Sacred Pipe is found.

THE GIVING OF THE PIPE

The powerful Sacred Pipes are not simply made by people, they are given, at least in spirit, by the powerful beings to individuals, bands, societies, or the tribe as a whole. They may have been given in mythic time or in memory time. For the former there are myths of long standing; for the latter, accounts from memory that have a mythic quality because they concern spiritual beings. These accounts concern trance experiences, either visions or lucid dreams, at times sought through fasting or the sun dance, at times unsought. In this section, a synopsis of myths from four traditions will be presented: Blackfoot, Gros Ventre,

Crow, and Lakota. Two of these myths were related to the recorder by those desiring (Garter Snake and Black Elk) to preserve them for their people, and another two were told by those with proprietary rights to the myth (Brings-Down-the-Sun and Foolish Man).

Blackfoot

In the previous chapter, the Medicine Pipes were discussed. George Bird Grinnell (1908:113–116) has a story (not necessarily the myth) of a Medicine Pipe in his collection of Blackfoot tales.

The story is placed in mythic time. Thunder comes and strikes a married couple sitting in their lodge. When the man revives, he finds his wife missing. He thinks she has gone about her chores but begins to worry when she has not returned by sunset. He searches the camp and questions those he meets, but she is missing. He then realizes that Thunder has stolen her.

He leaves the village for the hills to mourn her loss. When day comes, he sets out to find Thunder's abode. He questions the animals he encounters but all warn him against his quest and urge him to return to his people. Finally, after many months, he encounters Raven Chief living in an unusual dwelling, a stone tipi.

Raven welcomes him and offers food. When the man tells of his quest, Raven warns him that Thunder lives nearby, also in a stone lodge. Inside are hung the eyes of all those he has killed or abducted. To assist the man in regaining his wife, Raven gives him two "medicines." The first is a raven's wing, which if pointed at Thunder will force him backward, the second, an arrow with an elkhorn shaft that will shoot through Thunder's stone lodge.

The man goes to Thunder's lodge, enters and sits by the doorway. Thunder threatens the man, who then points the raven wing at Thunder. Thunder falls backward on his bed, quivering, but soon recovers. (One is reminded here of the effect of the *megis* shell in the Midewiwin ritual.) The man then shoots the magic arrow through the stone lodge, letting in a shaft of sunlight. Thunder concedes and allows the man to cut down his wife's eyes, which were hanging among the others from the top of the lodge. As soon as her eyes are cut down, she becomes alive, standing beside her husband.

Thunder says:

Now you know me. I am of great power. I live here in summer, but when winter comes, I go far south. I go south with the birds. Here is my pipe. It is medicine. Take it and keep it. Now when I first come in the spring, you shall fill and light this pipe, and you shall pray to me, you and all the people.

This was the origin of the first Medicine Pipe. (See fig. 5 for a pipe of a type common in Blackfoot usage with a Thunderbird engraved on one side and lightening on the other.)

Walter McClintock (1910:253) briefly presents a quite different version of the origin of the Medicine Pipe. In his version, Thunder strikes a man down. While he lies unconscious, Thunder appears in a vision, shows him the pipe, and says:

I have chosen you that I might give you this Pipe. Make another just like it. Gather together also a medicine bundle, containing the skins of the many animals and birds, which go with it. Whenever any of your people are sick, or dying, a vow must be made and a ceremonial given with a feast. The sick will then be restored to health.

McClintock (1910:423–426) was also told by Brings-down-the-Sun, son of Iron Shirt, a keeper of the Medicine Pipe bundle, the vision of his father that led to the addition of another pipe to the bundle.

Brings-down-the-Sun was camped with his father and grandfather on what is now called the St. Mary's River on the eastern slope of the Rockies in Montana. His father went to hunt meat and had trailed an elk to the timberline when he saw a herd of mountain sheep. Iron Shirt followed them up Chief Mountain. Near the summit, he came across a deep pit from which was issuing a thick, foul-smelling smoke. He tossed a stone down it, but could not hear it hit bottom. As he turned to leave, he faced a black cloud coming up the mountainside. There was a terrible crash and he fell to the ground.

Iron Shirt saw a woman standing over him. Her face was painted black with red zigzag lightning streaks below her eyes. Behind her was a man holding a large weapon, who said, "I told you to kill him at once, but you stand there pitying him." She chanted: "When it rains, the noise of the Thunder is my medicine." The man sang and fired his weapon, which sounded like a crash of thunder, and lightning flashed from the hole on the mountain peak.

Suddenly, Iron Chief found himself lying paralyzed inside a huge cavern and heard a voice saying, "This is the person who threw the stone into your fireplace." He heard the beating of a drum; after the fourth drumbeat, he was able to sit up. He saw the Thunderbird and his family. All of the children had drums painted with the Thunderbird's green talons and yellow lightning zigzags coming from a beak. The Thunderbird smoked his pipe, blowing two whiffs upward toward the sky and two whiffs toward the earth. At each whiff, the thunder crashed.

The Thunderbird spoke to Iron Chief:

> I am the Thunder Maker and my name is Many Drums. You have witnessed my great power and can now go in safety. When you return to your people, make a pipe just like the one you saw me smoking and add it to your bundle. Whenever you hear the first thunder rolling in the springtime, you will know that I have come from my cavern, and that it is time to take out my pipe. If you should ever be caught in the midst of a heavy thunderstorm and feel afraid, pray to me, saying, "Many drums! Pity me, for the sake of your youngest child," and no harm will come to you.

When Iron Chief returned from the mountain, he added a pipe similar to the one the Thunderbird smoked to the Medicine Pipe bundle. (The smoking of the pipe by Thunderbird was understood as an adoption ritual.)

White Clay People (Gros Ventre)

In 1941, at the age of seventy-three, Garter Snake (1980:103–122) told the myth and ritual for the chief medicine pipe of her people, the Feathered Pipe. Although she had become a Catholic, she had not, as had been expected, lost her affection and respect for the Pipe. She narrated the tradition so that it might be recorded and not lost forever with her death. Her father, Bull Lodge, had been keeper of the Pipe, and she had been ritually made the Pipe Child; the Pipe was her brother (see Cooper:II, 136). When she was a child, Bull Lodge told her this tradition so that, in the proper time, she would be able to exactly retell it. Bull Lodge's narration took a full night, from sunset to sunrise.

In essence, the origin of the Pipe begins with a man who, from age forty had a dream repeated every spring for four consecutive years. After the fourth dream, he spoke to the elders of his people and told them the dream. He had his lodge pitched to the west of the camp circle facing east; it was filled with his own possessions and contributions from his relatives. He sent the younger of his two wives and all the children to stay with her parents. It was late spring, the time of the Thunders.

He warned the people to prepare for a thunderstorm. In the early evening a severe thunderstorm arrived, and it rained all night. In the morning the man's lodge, belongings, and horses were all gone, but the ground was dry where the lodge had been, while all around the earth was soaked. The man and woman, naked but for their robes, were found sitting on a white bison robe facing east, the man to the left of his wife. He had four items in his hand: the Feathered Wand, the Pipe, the Whistle, and the Image, all otherworldly in appearance.

The couple was unmoving and silent, which everyone respected. A lodge was erected over them, and they moved without standing to the bed prepared for them facing east. They remained with their robes over their heads, the man holding the four sacred items.

> Around noon the man spoke: Relatives, I have received something for you and my people. This is life, and it will be with our people throughout all generations to come. I was given this Feathered Wand, this Pipe, this Whistle, this Image, and names for my wife and myself. I am to be called Man Whistles, and my wife is to be called Woman Goes First.

The sacred items were wrapped in the white bison robe. He told his people how to prepare the sweat lodge for which he had been given instructions and songs. After the sweat ceremony, he dreamed about the proper incense for the Pipe ceremony and for four subsequent sweat ceremonials, and that the Pipe was to be passed on to four consecutive owners. Over time, he had further dream instructions for additions to the Pipe, such as a specially prepared drum, and additional rituals, such as transfer ceremonies. The three subsequent owners also had dreams during fasts that continued the instruction.

Crow

William Wildschut was a businessman who lived near the Crow reservation in Montana. Between 1918 and 1927, a time of cultural and religious genocide, he obtained over 260 sacred bundles from the Crow for the collection of George G. Heye, now the Museum of the American Indian in New York City. Along with some of the bundles, he received the "story" of the Medicine Pipe Society's pipe from Foolish Man, the leader of the society. (See figure 6 for a pipe from a sacred bundle collected by Wildschut.)

This myth illustrates another of the common means of receiving a pipe, either by gift from, or courageous exploit against, another people. For example, the Circle Dance Pipe of the Blackfoot was brought back as a gift from the Arapaho (Schaeffer, n.d.). The Crow myth illustrates the taking of a pipe from a traditional enemy with the aid of a powerful being, here Bison. This means of obtaining a pipe is parallel to the way the Blackfoot obtained a Medicine Pipe from Thunder with the aid of the spirit, Raven. A summary of the myth follows (Wildschut:114–119).

In the distant past, at a time before the Crow separated from the Hidatsa, a war party of five men and a boy were defeated by the Sioux. When they failed to return, a young man in love with the boy's sister and his friend went to seek them. The two came upon the remains of the five warriors and realized that the boy had been captured.

That night the young man went to sleep using as a pillow a bison skull that still had its hair and horns. He dreamed that a man descended from the sky, making four stops. At each halt, he smoked a pipe. When he reached the young man, he spoke to him holding the pipe in both hands:

> This is the medicine pipe. Since it came from the sky it must never touch the ground. The blue beads on the stem represent the sky; the white tassels are the streaky clouds bringing rain, and the red tassels, the red clouds of the evening sunset. A duck-head is placed on the stem because when the Great Spirit made the earth it was the duck which brought the first mud from the bottom of the waters which grew into the earth. Owl feathers should be attached to the pipe, because the owl is a great medicine bird. It can see in the dark and into the future. Eagle feathers should also be represented, because the eagle is the chief of the birds. It is the most powerful, can fly the highest, and yet it can see everything that happens on earth . . . and with the pipe there shall always be an ear of corn, because corn represents the first fruit of the earth.

The next morning the two friends continued on their journey and reached a large Sioux camp where the Sun Dance was taking place. At night they sneaked into the encampment and finally found the captured boy tied, as an offering, to the top of the Sun Dance lodge in the middle of the camp. On his way back out, he captured two horses and gave one to his friend to ride back to their home, while he would remain to rescue the boy or die in the attempt.

In the depth of the night, he again made his way into the enemy encampment and was able to reach the boy, cut him down and carry him out of the lodge. Eventually they were spotted and he ran into a tipi. There he found a pipe bundle exactly like the one he saw in his dream. He sat down with the boy still on his back and the bundle in his arms.

When the Sioux warriors rushed into the tipi and saw him holding the medicine pipe bundle, they held back from killing him. After a council, the Sioux gave them food and water and told them that if the young man succeeded in two difficult trials, they would be free. Succeeding, the young man returned to his people with the boy and the medicine pipe.

In the ceremony of this pipe (Wildschut 1975:190–120), a bison skull is placed facing the rising sun. A feast is prepared, representing the food given the two Crows by their enemy. Part of the food is offered to the four directions, the earth (Wildschut's narrative is confused here), the sun, the pipe, the feathers, and the buffalo skull. The offering is placed inside the skull. The pipe is then filled and smoked in the traditional way, with sacred songs.

Lakota (Sioux)

In 1896, James R. Walker, who had long experience with and interest in Native people, became the physician of the Pine Ridge Reservation in the Dakotas. From then until 1914, he spent his free time learning from the Lakota men their religious traditions and understanding, recorded in notes recently published (1980) and his own publication (1917). In his notes are two versions of how the tribal Sacred Pipe, the Bison Calf Pipe, was obtained one from Finger and another from Thomas Tyron (Walker 1980:109–112, 148–150). In the late 1940s, at the end of his life, Black Elk, an Oglala elder, related to Joseph Epes Brown the tribal rituals, so that they would be recorded and preserved for his people. His narration (1953:3–9) begins with the fundamental holy act for his people, the giving of the Bison Calf Pipe. All these versions agree in their essential details; the following is a synopsis of the two versions.

In the mythic past, two young men were on a hill scouting ahead of their band. Far off they saw a young woman coming toward them. She was covered only by her hair, as long as a robe, and she was carrying something. One of the young men decided to meet her in hopes of a sexual encounter. The other warned him that the woman might be a sacred being, that she might be a bison woman who would take him back to her people. But his friend was not afraid and did not heed the advice. When the young man approached her, a cloud covered them both. When the cloud lifted, the youth was but a pile of bones.

The young woman called to the other young man and told him he would not be harmed as long as he treated her with respect. She had brought something for his people, and he was to warn them to prepare for her coming. She then disappeared in a mist, and the youth knew she was a sacred being.

His people prepared a feast. When it was ready she appeared in their midst. She served the feast to the children, the women, and then to the men. She then bade the men look up, and they saw a beautiful woman. She brought forth a pipe, filled it in the sacred manner, took several puffs and passed it to the chief. After he smoked, she instructed him to pass it around the circle. She told the people that this pipe was for them and they could make others like it. As long as they kept this pipe, she would help them. She would always be present in the smoke of the pipe, and take their prayers to the powerful sacred beings in intercession.

The Lakota have ever since preserved this pipe, calling it the Bison Calf Pipe and considering it their holiest object. A highly respected elder, Lame Deer, tells of the time he was able to unwrap this pipe and another associated with it:

I held the pipes. The bowls were my flesh. The stem stood for all the generations. I felt my blood going into the pipe, I felt it coming back. I felt the pipes coming alive in my hands, felt them move. I felt a power surging from them into my body, filling all of me. Tears were streaming down my face . . . I knew that within this pipe were all the powers of nature, that within this pipe was me. I knew that when I smoked the pipe I was at the center of all things, giving myself to the Great Spirit. . . . (Lame Deer and Erdoes 1972:252–53)

PIPE AND TOBACCO IN COSMOGONIC MYTHS

Western religions, with a linear sense of time, emphasize beginnings. Time is considered finite. God is that which exists before time and creates not only the world, but time itself. Hence, the Christian Bible begins with the Genesis of the world and ends with the Revelations of its apocalyptic end. But Native American thought, as that of many other non-Western cultures, did not consider time finite and did not, prior to synthesis with Christian ideology, emphasize creation. Rather, Native myths focus on the movement of the people to where they are, either the horizontal movement of migration (e.g., Apache, Ojibwa), or the vertical movement of emergence from realms beneath this world (e.g., Hopi, Navajo).

Creation, when it is dealt with at all, tends to occur in the context of narratives about the "culture hero," the spiritual being who helps the people attain the necessities for life and culture. In many of these myth cycles, the culture hero re-creates the earth after a deluge express-ing the "earth-diver" motif: animals bring up mud from the bottom of the sea that grows into the land on which we live. The Biblical flood account is a remnant of this common mythic theme.

Unlike the Sacred Pipe origin myths, the following cosmogonic myths, except for the Winnebago, were not told by those with the right to narrate them. Even when the Winnebago myth was imparted to Radin, there was great resentment by many Winnebago against the informant. Hence, these recordings tend to be fragmentary and con-fused.

The Giving of Tobacco

The circumstances surrounding Radin's recording of Winnebago reli-gious traditions were discussed in the preceding chapter. From 1908 to 1909, he was able to record in its entirety the oral tradition of the Medicine Lodge (1945:27–28). In the preliminary myth, concerning origins, we have the mythic account of the giving of tobacco:

> Again our grandmother, Earth, arose and said, "Did you wish to know how I was to help you, Grandson [the culture-hero Hare]? Well, look at me. Earthmaker had me bring what I shall now show you so that the human beings will have something with which to ask for life." Then she opened her body where her heart was and, suddenly, very green leaves

were to be seen there, the shape of an ear. It was tobacco. It was white as a blossom. Then she opened her body on the right side and, again, she spoke, "Grandson, look at me!" There, unexpectedly, ears of corn were to be seen. "These Earthmaker had me bring you for your uncles and your aunts." Soon a stalk became visible whose leaves were very green and whose tassels were white. It was the corn which was to become our food.

This mythic fragment indicates that for the Winnebago, as for other Native people, communication with the spiritual powers, the function of tobacco, is the primary condition for life; it comes before food itself. Similarly, in Cherokee myths, we find that tobacco is obtained or brought back to the people in the context of people dying without it (Mooney 1900:254–255).

In this regard, tobacco and the Sacred Pipe are synonymous. Among the Osage, the Crawfish Clan ritual also links the pipe to food and life itself:

> It (the pipe) shall also be the means by which they may obtain food
> When they use it as a means to obtain food
> They shall enable themselves to live to see old age as they travel the path of life. (La Flesche 1921:128)

The Giving of the Sacred Pipe

Within a Plains Cree creation myth, recorded by Verne Dusenberry (1962:66), after the first man and woman are created, they are given the gift of the Pipe:

> "My children,"the [Manitou] said, "I am going far away. I am going up where nobody will see me. However, I am leaving you certain things— main things that are very important. There will be four of them: Fire, Pipe [bowl], Pipe stem, and sweetgrass.
> "If, in the future, you wish to make any connection with me, these are the things to be used. And they must be used in this order: First, upward, in memory of your Creator; next, to the spirits of the four directions; and lastly, to Mother Earth."

Hence, the Sacred Pipe is the first gift to the original couple from the spirit realm (see fig. 23 for a Plains Cree Sacred Pipe).

The Pipe in the Re-creation of the Earth

In the Ojibwa version of the Algonkian re-creation myth, the deluge was caused by the attempt of the underwater spirits to kill Nanabush [Hare] after he killed their chief in revenge for the death of his brother Wolf. Nanabush saves the people and sends diving animals to bring up mud to re-create the land.

In the collected Gros Ventre versions, the reason for the deluge is either not known (Cooper 1957:II, 435–437), or the culture-hero himself caused the deluge to exterminate the people (Kroeber 1907a:59–61). This and several other details, including the emphasis on the number three instead of the Native American sacred number four, indicates influence from the Biblical version. However, the Gros Ventre myth, especially the earlier version in Kroeber, is of particular interest here because of the role of the Pipe.

Before causing the deluge, the culture-hero Nix'a^{n}t hung the "chief pipe" from a tripod (in the Arapaho version, a platform supported by four poles [Carter 1938:73]). Under each foot of the tripod, and under himself, he placed a chip of dried bison dung. For this reason he and the pipe floated. Above him flew Crow, frequently resting on the Pipe. Tired of sitting on the bison chip, Nix'a^{n}t cried. Finally he unwrapped the Pipe, which contained all the animals. Large Loon and then Small Loon failed to reach the bottom. Then Nix'a^{n}t sung Turtle to life who, nearly dead, brought up some mud from the bottom. With this mud, Nix'a^{n}t recreated the land.

The abbreviated Hidatsa re-creation myth that Bowers (1965:298–302) published indicates the conflation of several traditions. It combines two types of origin myths, earth-diver re-creation and emergence from realms below and has, as well, two culture-heroes. When the land was under water both culture heroes, First Creator [Coyote] and Lone Man, meet. Together they send down Goose, followed by Mallard, and then Teal, who all fail to bring up mud from the bottom. Finally Mud Hen succeeds. From this mud the land was recreated.

First Creator causes the people, who were then living in a realm below this land, to emerge into this world by climbing up a vine. After this episode, there is mentioned that Lone Man had a wooden pipe (the pipe most sacred to the Hidatsa, as to the Arapaho, is a "flat pipe," not a separate-stemmed pipe—see figure 8), but did not know how to use it. First Creator then orders Male Bison to produce tobacco for the pipe. Although Bowers makes no mention of the pipe being given the people, one assumes that this took place in the actual myth.

The Sacred Pipe in Clan Origin Myths

Native American people generally understand themselves to be born into clans that have both social and ritual functions. In many cultures, the clans have sacred bundles and origin myths. In 1914, within that long period when the U.S. and Canadian governments forcibly backed the Christian missionary demand that Native people not be allowed to practice their religion, Alanson Skinner obtained a number of clan Sacred Pipe bundles from the Iowa (see Appendixes). He also obtained from Chief David Tohee, in 1914, a summary of the Black Bear clan origin myth in which the Sacred Pipe plays a central role (Skinner 1926: 218–219). The following is a synopsis of the summary.

At the beginning of time, a man fasted for a vision under an elm tree. Four bears came out of the ground. They told the faster that they would give him power, and that they would become people. The fasting man then saw in a vision the events of the bears' journey after they left him.

They heard a distant pounding, and the one bear sent to investigate reported seeing a very old man working at something. Sent again to investigate, the bear found that the white-haired man had disappeared. They all rushed to the spot and found only a pipe bowl in the shape of a man. They took the pipe bowl with them.

They came to a river where a stick was floating upright. On it were streamers of blue or green seaweed or moss (symbolized by quillwork on subsequent pipestems). The eldest of the bears took it for the pipestem.

As they continued on, they met the four ancestors of the Bison clan. These brothers offered their pipe to the bears who reciprocated. (This meeting is given as the origin of the Iowa custom of splitting tribal leadership between the Bison and Bear clans.)

While a feast was being prepared by both parties, the eldest bear was so hungry that when he seized the pipe in his mouth, he split the stem. To cover his embarrassment, he gave himself the name "Splitting the Pipestem," a name that continued to be used within the clan.

PIPESTONE

Stone pipebowls are made of tan, grey, green, black, and red stone, but the latter two predominate. All pipe-using cultures utilized both, but there are cultural preferences. For example, the Blackfoot and Arapaho prefer black for most ceremonies. In many cultures the color black symbolizes Earth. Throughout the growing season, a Mandan priest smoked a black Sacred Pipe (Will and Hyde 1917:263). Red has symbolized the life-force for over fifty thousand years, as evidenced by Neanderthal burials, and still maintains this meaning for modern cultures, such as the Chinese.

Red pipebowls are favored by the Lakota and Dakota, some of whom lived and still live by one of the few sites where red stone is found in southwestern Minnesota. In English, the stone is known as catlinite, after George Catlin, who is often thought to be the first who wrote about the site, although several other Euro-Americans actually preceded him by a few years (Murray 1963). He recorded (Catlin 1844:II, 168) the following myth:

> That in the time of a great freshet, which took place many centuries ago, and destroyed all the nations of the earth, all the tribes of the red men assembled on the Coteau de Prairie, to get out of the way of the waters. After they had all gathered here from all parts, the water continued to rise, until at length it covered them all in a mass, and their flesh was converted into red pipe stone. Therefore it has always been considered neutral ground—it belongs to all tribes alike, and all were allowed to get it and smoke it together.
>
> While they were all drowning in a mass, a young woman, K- wap-tah-w, caught hold of the foot of a very large bird that was flying over, and was carried to the top of a high cliff, not far off, that was above the water. Here she had twins, and their father was the war-eagle, and her children have since peopled the earth.
>
> The pipe stone, which is the flesh of their ancestors, is smoked by them as the symbol of peace, and the eagle's quills decorates the head of the brave.

Here we have aspects of an origin myth that combines people and red pipestone.

"ALL MY RELATIONS": THE THEOLOGY
OF THE SACRED PIPE

The most sacred myths are told in the context of a smoke offering, often with drum and rattles. The ritual context creates a sacred time and space; it connects present time and mythic time. Hence, what has been related in the preceding are not the myths themselves, but synopses of the narratives, which are but a small part of the mythic complex. However few and fragmentary the relevant mythic narratives that have been recorded, there is sufficient information to understand the role of the Sacred Pipe in the religious understanding of Native people.

Tobacco and the Pipe were given to humans at the very beginning of their existence. In the Winnebago Medicine Lodge myth, tobacco was given to people even before the staple of subsistence, corn. For the Cree, the Sacred Pipe complex (fire, pipebowl with tobacco, pipestem, and sweetgrass) was the parting gift to the people from the Creator. In the Gros Ventres re-creation myth, the Pipe was central to both the formation of the world and the release of the game animals. In the Hidatsa merging of Caddoan and Siouan traditions, the Pipe and tobacco were present at the emergence of the people onto the newly re-created earth. According to the Iowa Black Bear clan origin myth, the first items received by the bears after they came out of the earth were first a pipebowl and then a pipestem.

The Sacred Pipe is essential for life, because it is with tobacco smoke offered through fire or the medium of the Pipe that humans can pray for the necessities of life from the more powerful beings. For this reason, La Flesche (1921:61) interprets the Osage ritual affirmation, "I am a person who has made of a pipe his body," to mean that the pipe is the "life symbol" of the people. Pipes were and are given to individuals by these beings for use by families, clans, societies and whole tribes. Through the medium of the Pipe, people can heal the sick, control the weather, ask the animals to give themselves to the people for food, and harm their enemies and make peace. The gift of the Pipe from the powerful beings allow humans in turn to offer the gift of tobacco smoke to these and other beings.

The myths described above enable us to begin to understand these powerful and helpful beings; they allow an analysis of Native American "theology." The term must be used with caution, because Native spiritual beings, unlike the Western deity, are not supernatural, that is, beyond nature, but rather are fully natural beings; there is no absolute distinction between creator and created. All beings are relations; hence, the spirits, including animals, plants, and minerals, are all addressed by humans as "Grandfather," "Grandmother," "Mother" and "Father." This connection is often given verbal affirmation at the conclusion of sweat lodge ceremonials and the smoking of the Sacred Pipe when the participants may individually state, "All my relations." Hallowell's now classic "other-than-human persons" still best distinguishes this understanding.

A related issue is whether "theology" or "theologies" is most appropriate. Among the large number of tribes using the separate-stemmed pipe in North America, a common theology, as well as a common cosmology, is found, even among cultures of different language families. Details may differ, but there is a similar structural relationship between other-than-human persons and humans. This is why Sacred Pipes and bundles may come from another people, either as a gift or by capture, which in this mode is a gift from the spirits, as in the Crow myth.

This theological similarity exists despite the means by which theological understanding develops. Being experiential, understanding is based on and open to continual revelation from the spirits themselves. Hence, Native theology is flexible and able to rapidly respond to changing circumstances without altering its fundamental characteristics. Revelation takes place during ecstatic religious experience resulting from the rituals of fasting, sweat lodge and self-sacrifice (e.g., the sun or thirst dances), and lucid dreams. Since continuing revelation takes place within a mythic and ritual context, it maintains rather than disrupts religious continuity.

The theology of the Sacred Pipe is not, in itself, due to the influence of Christianity as Father Steinmetz has suggested (1984:68): "The religious meaning of the Sacred Pipe and its sacramental use has been influenced by Christianity, I believe, far more than most anthropologists are willing to admit." Steinmetz has correctly pointed to the importance of the Christian backgrounds of George Sword and Black Elk on the development of Lakota ideology, a development analyzed by Clyde Holler (1984,1984a). But, as I have argued in a previous study (1983), it is the very ritual and understanding of the Sacred Pipe that distinguishes the aboriginal concepts from the Christian overlay. The modification that did take place was a Native means of responding to Christian domination in order to preserve Native spirituality. The Sacred

Pipe as a vessel for sacrificial offering allows for synthesis with Christianity; but the significance of the Pipe existed not only long before Christianity came to the Americas, but even before Christianity began (see Chapter 5).

From the myths and rituals of the Sacred Pipe one can functionally distinguish four categories of spiritual beings: primary spirits, effective spirits, originating spirits, and instructive spirits. These categories are solely for analytical purposes; in actuality they overlap.

Primary Spirits

As discussed in the preceding chapter, the basic ritual of the Sacred Pipe indicates the primary spiritual recipients. While the primary spirits are central to rituals, it is their effective associations and symbols that are of mythic import. When directly referred to in myth, the primary spirits have become distant, as is Manitou of the Cree creation myth, or they are the source of life itself, as is Earth in the Winnebago Medicine Lodge creation myth.

Christian influence can be observed in the above two examples only as secondary features. In the Winnebago myth, the female Earth is subservient to the male Earthmaker, because Sky had become conflated with the Judeo-Christian Yahweh. By the time the myth was recorded, the Winnebago had been forced into a patrilineal and patriarchal social structure by the United States government. Hints of an earlier matrilineal structure can be found in the phrase, "your uncles and your aunts;" in matrilineal and matrilocal cultures, the individual's relationship with uncles and aunts is as strong as that with the natal parents. While the term "Manitou," which had functioned as a generic term for all spirits, came to signify only Sky in Cree religion, Manitou(= Creator) remains ritually equal to Earth; this is also true of the term, "Great Spirit," common since the mid-eighteenth century. However, when used in and of themselves, the terms "Great Spirit" and "Creator" refer to the reality beyond the spirits in their individual symbolic identities, to the life-force that gives rise to all existence.

The primary spirits can be divided into two categories: Earth and Sky, and the Four Directions. Mother or Grandmother Earth and Father or Grandfather Sky are often found in myths represented by their symbols. As specific celestial beings, they are, respectively, Grandmother or Mother Moon and Grandfather or Father Sun; as theriomorphic spirits,

they are Bear (Earth), Owl (Moon), and Eagle (Sun); as elemental spirits, they are Water and Fire. In some cultures, such as the Pawnee,
there are the additional celestial symbols of the Evening (female) and
the Morning (male) Stars.

Earth and Sky together form the powers of creation. The second
aspect of the primary spirit, the Four Directions or Winds, are the
power- and life-giving forces of the created. They represent the world
around us, the progression of the day, the rotation of the seasons, and
the stages of life. Symbolized by colors, animals, and plants, these
details vary from culture to culture, even subculture to subculture.

Effective Spirits

The effective spirits are those to whom the Sacred Pipe may be offered
after it has been offered to the primary spirits (the ritual order itself
varies), and they are the givers of most named Pipes. Hence, they are of
both ritual and mythic significance. These spirits may be symbolic of
the primary spirits as well. These are the other-than-human persons
from whom people may directly seek help, usually with the Pipe. There
are many of these spirits; almost every animal has its spiritual aspect.
Among the most important are Thunderbird, Bear, Bison, and Eagle.

In the Blackfoot and Gros Ventre origin myths of the Medicine
Pipe, the giver is Thunderbird, who also gave a supplementary pipe to
the Blackfoot bundle. The Thunderbird may also be a semi-
theriomorphic symbol of the West Wind. Thunderbird not only con-
trols severe and potentially destructive weather as in these myths, but
he can pass the power of the lightning flash to the warrior. The medicine pipe bundle of Standing Bull, the nineteenth-century Crow chief,
centers on a straight pipe bowl with the Big Dipper inscribed on one
side and a zigzag lightning flash on the other (fig. 6). "The pointing of
this pipe toward the enemy by the leader of the Crow war party was
thought to cause death just as surely as would a stroke of lightning"
(Wildschut 1975:122).

Bear gave its skin for the wrapping of the Blackfoot Medicine Pipe
(McClintock 1910:253). Bear, especially Grizzly Bear, can symbolize
ferocious protective power, but as a healing spirit, Bear, particularly
Black Bear, represents the renewing power of Earth. Every winter, Earth
sleeps under her blanket of snow; rejuvenated in the spring, she sends
forth the shoots of new life. So, too, Bear buries herself inside Earth for

her winter fast and comes forth in the spring with new life, her cubs. In the Iowa Black Bear clan origin myth, the four Bears come out of Earth. Hence, Bear is the most powerful of the healing spirits. The winged corollary of Bear is Owl, the powerful bird of the female night, important to both the Blackfoot and Crow Medicine Pipes referred to above.

One of the effects of Christian domination is that these beneficial effective spirits have come to be understood as evil. Except for the male spirit Sky, Christian missionaries tended to consider all other Native spirits, especially female ones, to represent the Devil. In Ojibwa culture, the healing spirit Bear came to be understood as associated with sorcery; hence, the term "Bear-walking" for the practice of evil power. Also in a number of cultures, Owl came to be understood as a symbol for death, rather than as a means for communication with departed relations (Hoffman 1891:171) or other beneficent powers.

Bison has female and male attributes. As Bull, Bison symbolizes warrior power. In the Hidatsa creation myth, Male Bison produced tobacco for the pipe. (In Hidatsa and related cultures, while women did all gardening for food, men grew tobacco.) But more important is the female aspect of Bison. She provided the peoples of the Plains with most of their meat and fat, their bone tools, their bison hide tipi covers, blankets and moccasins, and their sinew for sewing clothes. Without her there is no human life. And she gave the Lakota their tribal pipe and is "the spirit of the pipe" (Walker 1980:221). Bison, like Bear, is understood as emerging from the Earth (Walker, 1980:144).

In the origin myth of the Waterbuster Clan bundle of the Hidatsa (Bowers 1965:467–471), the Eagle spirits fulfill their mission to help the people by giving them a pipe, a pipe that killed their enemies, brought the rain when needed, called the bison, and healed the sick. Eagle is the winged spirit of the day sky, of the Sun. Soaring high in the sky, he sees all that happens in the world. His feathers on a pipestem sends our prayers to Father Sky, to Grandfather Sun, as Owl's feathers do to Mother Earth and Grandmother Moon.

Originating Spirits

The originating spirits re-create the world after the flood (usually in an earth-diver context), guide the emergence from one world to another, release the game animals, give the people all those inventions required for subsistence, such as fire, and gives those things needed to spiritually live, such as the Sacred Pipe. In comparative terminology, they are the "culture-heroes." Generally, they have a major role in myths, but do not commonly figure in ritual. The major originating spirits include Coyote, Crow-Raven, Hare, and Spider. Each culture usually has but one originating spirit, although tales about it will be paralleled if not duplicated by tales of another originating spirit in a different culture.

In the Hidatsa creation myth summarized above, Coyote figures in both earth-diver re-creation stories and in the emergence of the people (a synthesis of what are usually two different approaches to understanding the beginning of human life on this world). After the emergence of the people and the gift of the Pipe by Lone Man, a second originating spirit, Coyote, orders Male Bison to produce tobacco for Lone Man's pipe.

The Pipe plays an even more important role in the re-creation myth of the Gros Ventre, for the originating spirit Nix'a^{n}t floated on the Pipe while re-creating the world, and the bowl of the Pipe was the repository of all the animals. This was the Pipe that he gave to the White Clay people. However, the Pipe plays a role in cosmogonic myth in only a few traditions; most myths of the giving of the Pipe involve effective and primary rather than originating spirits.

Instructive Spirits

The instructive spirits are identical with the originating spirits, but have a different, albeit complementary, role. They are the sacred buffoons, who teach the people proper social behavior through the trouble they get themselves into in their ribald escapades. From a comparative perspective, they are called "tricksters." Just as in their role as originating spirits, Spider, Hare, Crow-Raven, and Coyote as instructive spirits have a mythic but not a ritual function. From the first snowfall to the reappearance of the Thunders, the myths of the instructive spirits entertain the people during the long, dark winter nights. Through these humorous and entertaining myths, people learn the pitfalls of unnatural and unsocial behavior.

In summary, we learn from the myths the origin of the Sacred Pipes, usually gifts from the effective and originating spirits. The Pipe is the means for the people to communicate with the primary and effective spirits. The instructive spirits usually play no direct role in either pipe ritual or myth.

From the myths and rituals, we can understand that although the spirits are multiple, creation is a result of their unity. It is when the female and male spirits, symbolizing the polarities of spiritual energy, are joined together that the world and life itself come into being.

Furthermore, life is not necessary; it is a gift from the spirits. From them we receive not only the gift of life, but the gift of food and other necessities of life, including the Sacred Pipe. All relationships involve the exchange of gifts. With tobacco and Pipe, we can express our gratitude to the spirits for their gifts by offering smoke.

IV

Description and Symbolism

TYPES OF PIPES

As discussed in the first chapter, there are different types of pipes for offering tobacco, of which the separate-stemmed pipe is but one. These variations affect both religious use and understanding; ignorance of these distinctions has led to misunderstandings.

Tubular Pipes

The most basic type of pipe is a simple tube with tobacco placed in one end and the smoke sucked out of the other (figs. 9–11). This type of pipe is related to tubes for sniffing tobacco snuff and tubes used in healing rituals in which the healer sucks the sickness from the patient's body into the tube. It has been suggested that the shamanic sucking tube is the progenitor of the tubular smoking pipe (Birket-Smith 1929:37–39). Tubular pipes were used throughout the Americas in the past, and continue in ritual use in the western part of North America.

Usually tubular pipes are wider at the tobacco end than at the mouthpiece (fig. 9). To prevent tobacco from being sucked into the smoker's mouth, a small stone may be placed in the bowl part, allowing the passage of smoke around it but preventing particles of ash and tobacco from continuing down the tube.

The most common substance for tubular pipes is stone, sometimes with a slim, round bone mouthpiece. Pipes made from the leg bones of antelope or deer continued to be ritually smoked in the Plains into the twentieth century by the Arapaho, Cheyenne, Kiowa, Lakota, and Piegan (fig. 10). The bone pipes are usually wrapped with rawhide or sinew to prevent the bone splitting from the heat of the burning tobacco. Ceramic tubular pipes, along with stone ones, are also used in Pueblo rituals (fig. 11) and were made in the Southeast as well. In California, wooden tubular pipes were used, sometimes with a bowl insert of stone. Also found on islands off the coast of California are stone tubular pipes with inlaid shell decor, some sculptured to represent powerful sea spirits such as killer whale, giant ray and shark (see Burnett 1944).

Tubular pipes suffer several drawbacks. Small one are hard to hold without burning the fingers and may be fitted with a leather strap to serve as a handle (fig. 11). More important, to prevent the tobacco from falling out, they must be smoked with the head tilted back. This difficulty was resolved by bending the pipe so that the bowl pointed upward. That tubular pipes continue in ritual use despite these inconveniences indicates the sacred nature of past traditions for some cultures.

One-piece Elbow Pipes

Bending the pipe allowed gravity to keep the tobacco in the pipe with the smoker's head at the normal, most comfortable, angle. The development of pottery allowed the tube to be bent before the clay hardened, but pipes could also be made of stone by drilling from two directions, the holes meeting at an angle. Pipes excavated in a ritual context along the coast of California illustrate the transition from tubular to elbow pipes, beginning with a slight curve bending the bowl upward to the sharp angle of the elbow pipe (Burnett 1944). Once the concept developed, the elbow pipe inspired many variations, some to be discussed in Chapter 5. Pottery elbow pipes were used throughout the pottery-making regions of both North and South America.

Bending the pipe also brought the bowl into the view of the smoker, encouraging developments in decor. When Europeans sailing up the St. Lawrence River and into Lake Ontario encountered Iroquoian-speaking peoples, they found them individually smoking pipes in council. These were one-piece elbow pipes, usually ceramic. Many were decorated with elaborate images on the bowls (see Rutsch 1973). Some scholars have speculated that these represented the guardian spirits of the individuals smoking the pipes (Mathews 1976, 1979).

The tribal "flat pipe" of the Hidatsa and the Arapaho are unusually long one-piece elbow pipes, made of either wood or stone (fig. 8). They are also unusual in that they are used in cultures that otherwise only use separate-stemmed pipes.

The Separate-stemmed Pipe

Besides bending the pipe, a second means of creating a pipe with an upward-directed bowl is to drill a stone from two directions, meeting in the middle, with a hollow wooden or reed stem inserted into one of the holes. Such pebble pipe bowls have been found over much of North America, from simple, plain bowls to those with elaborate decoration. Since this type of pipe is the focus of this book, its many variations will be described later in this chapter.

Miscellaneous Pipe Developments

Massive effigy pipes. Simple effigy pipes will be discussed in the section on symbolism. However, forming a small class of their own are a few massive effigy pipes, some weighing up to three kilograms, that have been excavated or found. It is assumed that these pipes rested on the ground while being smoked with a long stem, which was perhaps passed in a circle during ceremonies, the pipe turning as the stem was passed. These pipes are found in the lower Mississippi Basin and in the southeastern United States.

Multi-stemmed basin pipes. Also from the Southeast and relatively rare are round pipe bowls with from four to fourteen stem holes. Again it is assumed that these pipes were used in ceremonies with smokers sitting in a circle about the large bowl, each with their own stem.

Tomahawk Pipes. Among the most desired early trade items from Europeans were metal axes of brass, iron, or steel. Eventually Europeans modified a slim axe, called "tomahawk" to approximate the word for the war club in Algonkian languages, by adding a pipe bowl opposite the blade. When fitted with a drilled shaft, this war axe could also serve as a pipe. Many were traded to Native people and more elaborate ones were given as treaty presents. In some instances, Native peoples used these pipes in their own treaty ceremonies. At the Grand Council of 1840 between the Ojibwa and Six Nations (Iroquois peoples), near present-day Toronto, one of the Christian Ojibwa chiefs used an elaborate tomahawk pipe given his nephew, the Ojibwa Methodist minister Peter Jones, two years earlier in England (Smith 1984). Because pipes cut from catlinite became tourist items in the late nineteenth century, a number a number of tomahawk pipes were made in this fragile stone.

Northwest Coast Pipes. Contact with Europeans led the Native people of the British Columbia coast to add their distinctive designs to nontraditional items for the purpose of trade. Elaborate pipes of argillite were carved as decorative items rather than for smoking.

DESCRIPTION OF THE SACRED PIPE

Typology

The various shapes of the Sacred Pipe or separate-stemmed pipe can be categorized in a number of ways. The categories used here were chosen both for convenience and because they will facilitate the historical discussion in Chapter 5. It should be understood that these categories are not Native ones. There are four basic shapes, each subject to a number of variations: elbow, keel, disc, and straight.

1a. Elbow. The elbow pipe is essentially a bent pipe, with the bowl bent at an angle, usually a right angle, to the stem (figs. 1, 13, 38). The bowl may be straight (fig. 45), curved (fig. 43), double-tapered (fig. 12), or conical (fig. 51), being wider at the top. The base may be round, square, or multisided. Other than surface decor, decoration may include a rim at the top of the bowl or a flange projecting from the top of the stem. The flange may have notches along the top or one or more holes. One hole may be used for a thong to connect the bowl to the stem, preventing the bowl from falling off during ceremonial use, which may include dancing. Some elbow pipes from the Northwest have a slight protrusion descending from the base with a hole from which sacred items may be suspended.

1b. Elbow: slight-projection and pointed-projection. At the bowl end of the elbow pipe, the base may slightly protrude past the bowl. Originally this may have been a slight knob (fig. 45). This protrusion developed into either a pointed projection (fig. 14), or a slight projection that may be rounded (fig. 16) or flat (fig. 37,40). Rounded projections may have a slight upturn (fig. 6).

1c. Elbow: double-bowl. An uncommon variation of the elbow pipe with slight or pointed projection is a pipe with a double bowl, i.e., two separate bowls on a single stem (fig. 17). Various reasons for this development will be discussed below under symbolism.

1d. Elbow: long-projection. A rare archaic variation, to be distinguished from the T-shape, is an elbow pipe with a projection as long as the stem end, often with a flange (figs. 7, 18). Both ends taper towards the bowl in the middle. The base is square and the projection usually increases towards an axe- shaped end. The bowl tends to have a double taper. (See Chapter 5 for discussion.)

1e. T The T-shape is similar to the long-projection elbow pipe without the rise at either end (figs. 22, 23, 41, 44). The bowl is straight or has the slightest double taper or rim (fig. 4). Hence, the shape is similar to an inverted T. Stem and bowl may be quite long. This shape has been misleadingly called Siouan, but nearly all Sacred Pipe-using cultures have used such pipes ritually since they were first developed in the second half of the nineteenth century (see Chapter 5).

1f. Elbow: effigy. A final variation of the elbow pipe has the bowl in the shape of an animal body (fig. 18) or head, or a human head (figs. 19, 20). The significance of these designs will be discussed in the section on symbolism.

2. Keel. The keel shape probably developed from the nugget shape. Some of the early vasiform shapes had an extension on the bottom, usually with a single hole (fig. 44). This developed into a style with a short round or rectangular base from which a bowl, usually with a pronounced double taper, projected at the top, and a projection of varying size and shape descended from the bottom (figs. 24, 26). In some cases, there may be no bottom projection at all. There may be one or more holes at the end of the bottom projection, or "keel". As the design developed, in some examples the ends of the base developed a curved sweeping upturn on the inside. In eastern versions, some projections indicate influence from the tomahawk pipe, having an axe-shaped projection (fig. 45). In the far Northeast, the pipes have a tall conical bowl and a brief keel with a single hole (fig. 25). This entire genre of pipes has been given the misleading name of Micmac, although its range is quite extensive (see Chapter 5), leading one group of scholars to wonder what Micmacs were doing in the Plains (Wallace and Forbes 1963). Micmac examples are actually quite rare.

3a. Disc. The disc shape is an archaic one typified by a wide horizontal rim at the top of the bowl (figs. 24-26). The bowl itself is quite narrow and shallow; even the large ones hold little tobacco. They vary in size from some of the smallest known Sacred Pipes to the largest (excluding the massive effigy pipes). The bowl rests on a round or rectangular base that may or may not project past the bowl. Some projections have four rounded points at the end or four grooves on the top.

3b. Circular. A second type of circular pipe, relatively uncommon, is vertical (figs. 27, 28). The pipes are slab sided and either a simple circle or a round bowl resting on a base with a slight projection. In the latter form, they are a version of the elbow pipe.

4. Straight. The straight pipe is a tubular pipe used with a stem (figs. 3, 29, 30, 41). The stem end, rather than being tapered to fit the mouth, is left with a bore large enough for a stem insert. Often the pipe has a rim at the stem end; the bowl may be round or rectangular.

Substance

The majority of separate-stemmed pipe bowls are made of stone, although bowls have been made of clay, pewter, and wood. None of these have been found in a ritual context, but it is quite likely that on the East Coast, from Maryland southward, the majority of Sacred Pipe bowls were made of pottery at the time of contact. Pewter versions of stone bowls are occasionally found in the upper Mississippi Basin and Great Lakes area, as are wooden bowls, sometimes with a metal insert.

Stone bowls are most commonly made of black or red stone, with grey the third most common color. Some pipes are made of greenish or buff-colored stones. Black bowls are either of black stone per se, or of other colored stone, including red, that has been deliberately blackened over fire. (See fig. 2 for a partially blackened catlinite pipe.)

The red stone for pipe bowls is named "catlinite" in English after the painter and author George Catlin, who came across one of the major quarries in the 1830s in southwestern Minnesota. This quarry has since become a National Monument (see Murray 1965 for its history) and is a major source for both contemporary Native Sacred Pipes and tourist pipes. The stone tends toward a bright, medium-intense red with buff spots. It is found close to the surface in narrow horizontal sheets, which explains why pipes made from this quarry for the last century and a quarter tend to be narrow throughout. The fine-grained stone is soft when quarried, allowing for elaborate carving when desired. A darker red catlinite came from quarries in southern Wisconsin, and other, early catlinite quarries were in the Ohio Valley.

The black stones come from a number of places. In the western Great Lakes area, fine-grained, deep black steatite that allowed for elaborate carving was used.

Some red and black pipes had an inlay decoration. The material for inlay was most commonly lead, although pewter and German silver were also used (figs. 39–41). The stone was cut away for the design, the soft metal placed in the grooves, and the whole filed and sanded smooth. The metals were first obtained from items of European manufacture, including lead bullets, but by the eighteenth century, Native people were mining lead for such use in the upper Great Lakes, where they had been mining and manufacturing copper implements for thousands of years.

Stems are almost always made from wood, although some stems have been made from catlinite since the end of the nineteenth century (fig. 44). None of the latter appear in ritual use. Round stems are created by pushing out the pith, leaving a smoke channel in the center of the stem. The earliest extant stems are of this type, hence the term from the French, "calumet," meaning "reed." Flat stems are generally made by splitting the wood, gouging out a channel for the smoke, and then joining the two halves together with glue, sinew, or brass tacks. This method of making a flat stem allows for elaborate pierced designs, as well as for steaming to twist the stem into a spiral (fig. 22).

A favorite wood for stems, especially round and square ones, is sumac. The pith of sumac is very soft and relatively easy to push or burn out with a thin rod. Its distinctive branches have color layers from white on the outside, to yellow, to yellow-orange. Willow and red osier were also used for thin round stems. Flat stems are made from a variety of hardwoods, especially ash. During the 1960s and 1970s, most of the tourist pipes made in Pipestone, Minnesota, had stems made from California redwood obtained from a local lumber yard. However, the Pipestone pipemakers have recently begun to use sumac again.

Bowl Decoration

Bowl decoration is in part determined by the shape. For example, the largest disc pipes may have two triangles, with points toward the stem, on the anterior projection that flows from the disc (fig. 26). This decor is found on no other shape. Similarly, elbow pipes and their many variations may have a flange on the stem side of the base, leading to a number of possible decorative opportunities.

Flanges were originally quite small, beginning as a means of attaching a thong to secure the bowl to the stem when in use (figs. 2, 12, 21). Once the potential of the flange for decoration was realized, some became quite large (figs. 36, 37, 51). On some pipes the flanges are vestigial remnants without functional or major decorative importance (figs. 1, 17).

Flanges may have ridges on the top, one or more holes, incised border lines, decorative cutouts (figs. 36, 37) or inlay, or they may become converted to elaborate carvings. The latter were most likely made for Euro-American tastes, beginning among the Ojibwa in the late eighteenth century, the Pawnee in the early nineteenth century, the North Carolina Cherokee in the mid-nineteenth century, and the eastern Sioux in the late nineteenth century. Some of the Cherokee carvings have an erotic subject.

Other carvings infrequently occur on the projection of elbow pipes, particularly those made in the Southeast, and occasionally the bowls themselves are carved. Flat rims are found on the tops of some early bowls (fig. 13), and the stem ends of the base may be of a larger or different shape than the rest of the base. Grooves and ridges may be carved on both the stem ends of the base or the upper part of the bowl.

On some pipes made at Pipestone in the second half of the nineteenth century, an elaborate design was created by stippling around an outline. Finally, inlay was used to create both simple and elaborate designs. On some black pipes, both metal and catlinite, inlays were used to create a striking effect (fig. 39).

Keel pipes offer an opportunity for decoration on keels, bases, and bowls. The keels may have one or more holes and patterned ridges (fig. 26). The bowl may have incised lines or ridges. Some keel pipes of the elaborate style with upturned bases were elaborately inlaid with German silver and catlinite and hung with silver chains.

Straight bowls may have figures carved on them in relief as well as incised decoration (fig. 6). A rim of varying proportions, sometimes quilled or beaded, may be on the stem end of the bowl.

All pipes may have an incised design of sacred beings on the bowl, although this is rare. One of the earliest datable elbow pipes collected by a European (the circumstances of collection are unknown) has three spirit-animal figures incised in outline on the bowl (figs. 12, 44).

Stem Decoration

Stems range in size from a decimeter to well over a meter in length; the longer ones are more likely to have elaborate decoration. Most pipes, particularly those for which ritual use can be ascertained, are undecorated, except for a number that have been rubbed with red ochre (probably mixed with bear grease, as in fig. 29). Decorated stems may be carved and or decorated by the addition of quillwork, beads, ribbons, or parts of mammals and birds.

Carving of stems can be unique, inspired by individual visions, such as the Winnebago pipe illustrated (fig. 43), or more conventional, illustrating the maker's skill. The latter include flat stems with elaborate cutouts requiring an angled smoke channel ("puzzle" stems). Bark-covered stems may have the bark partly cut away in a pattern (fig. 45), or a simple grooved repeated pattern may be incised. Catlinite stems are often lathe-turned; their manufacture began with factories in Pipestone, Minnesota, turning out catlinite candlesticks. (A turn-of-the-century man-and-snake "effigy" catlinite candlestick is illustrated in Ewers 1986: fig. 205.)

The earliest wrapped decorations are dyed porcupine quills in circles around round stems (fig. 1). By the early eighteenth century, finely flat-braided porcupine quill wrapping began to appear, and by the late nineteenth century became standard on the first third of flat stems (fig. 44). Fur, bird necks and heads, horsehair, and ribbons or stroud (wool blanket material) may all be used in wrapping all or part of a stem. Parts of scalps, dyed horsehair, feathers, sometimes quilled, ribbons and strouding, and beaded thongs are among the materials that may be hung from or tied to decorated stems (fig. 42). Sweetgrass may be tied to undecorated stems or bowls (fig. 22), not for decoration, but rather for purification.

BOWL SYMBOLISM

Since at least the late eighteenth century, pipes have been made by Native people for trade to Euro-Americans. British Indian agents began collections of Native artifacts in the late eighteenth century. Major Jasper Grant, from 1806 to 1809 the commandant at Amherstberg (near present-day Windsor, Ontario), the major western frontier post for British North America, brought a number of pipes, including unsmoked ones, back to Ireland with him (Phillips 1984). In the early nineteenth century, a number of Euro-Americans, including the frontier artist George Catlin, collected a large number of pipes (Ewers 1986:15) of types seemingly not favored by Native peoples. None of these catlinite carved pipes is to be found in a ritual context, and a frequent subject is the "whiskey trade." The most elaborate nineteenth-century eastern inlaid pipes have a decor of playing cards (hearts, diamonds, clubs, and spades), indicating symbols favored by Euro-Americans, while western pipes tend to have romantic "Western" themes (fig. 41). One must question whether pipes considered sacred would have been sold or traded to non-Natives, excluding pipes presented to non-Native participants, before the religious repression of the reservation period. The following discussion of symbolism is limited to pipes with a definite or probable ritual function.

The Bowl

The bowl of the Sacred Pipe is in itself of major symbolic significance. Both hollows symbolize the female. The smoking end is a vessel for offering tobacco and is symbolically parallel with food vessels, usually made and used by women. The hole for receiving the stem symbolizes the vagina, which is symbolically (and linguistically in some languages) equated with Earth. The most awesome part of pipe ceremonies is when the two parts of the pipe are joined, when the male stem is inserted into the female bowl, at which time ritually significant pipes become potent. Those who have experienced these rituals will have noticed a profound hush falling over the participants at such moments.

The predominant colors of stone pipe bowls also relate to female symbolism. Although mythic details vary from culture to culture, red catlinite bowls, similar to red ochre, symbolize blood, the body's life fluid, or life itself. Life comes from the female, Earth or woman, and is visible, respectively, in water and menstrual blood. Black pipe bowls symbolize Earth itself. Stone or clay, the predominant substances of Sacred Pipe bowls, are of the earth as well. During the Arapaho Sun Dance, Earth is fertilized by smoking, in a black stone pipe, tobacco mixed with black paint pigment, symbolizing Earth, and red paint pigment, symbolizing "life-giving or fertilizing power" (Will and Hyde 1917:263).

Red and black bowls are approximately equal in number. Of the pipes studied that had had a definite or probable ritual use (see Appendix II), fifty-four percent were of red stone and forty-four percent were black or grey.

Double pipe bowls have varying interpretations for the symbolism of the two bowls. For the illustrated pipe (fig. 17), assuming Skinner's identification is correct, its manufacture was based on a vision; one bowl is to be used for settling internal strife and the other for making peace with other tribes (Skinner 1926: 218). For other such pipes, interpretations vary; examples include one bowl for war and one for peace, one bowl for day use and one for night use, and one bowl for hunting buffalo and one for making peace.

Decor

Most Sacred Pipe bowls are plain. Where there is decoration, it tends to be limited to circular ridges and incised circles, holes on flanges or keels, and cutouts on flanges. The symbolic significance often lies in the numbers, usually four or its double, eight, representing the Four Directions. Also of importance is the number six, representing the Four Directions, Earth and Heaven, and, especially among the Lakota, the number seven, which has several associations, including the Pleiades and the Big Dipper.

On inlaid pipes, circles with a pointed rim may represent the sun. The symbolism of disc and circular pipes is unclear because they may represent the sun or the earth; for black pipe bowls, it is probably the latter. Other symbols of astronomical or atmospheric significance are more certain. For example, the circular pits on some Crow straight pipes are in the form of the Big Dipper (fig. 17). The incised zigzag lines on these and other pipes symbolize lightning (fig. 6).

Effigy Orientation

Among the most interesting pipes from a sculptural perspective are those of animals or humans. These have engendered major misunderstandings, particularly about their placement and function. Ted Brasser (1980) has presented a most useful analysis of Native American decor, pointing out that the designs on moccasins were intended to be seen by the wearer and are so oriented; he has termed this placement "self-directed" decor. On one-piece Iroquoian pipes, the effigies face the smoker. Zena Mathews (1976) has convincingly argued that these particular effigies represent the smoker's guardian spirit. These pipes were not passed around the circle but were smoked individually (see Chapter 2).

Those apparently unfamiliar with the ritual of the Sacred Pipe have confused the ritual of the Iroquoian one-piece pipe with the separate-stemmed Sacred Pipe, to which Brasser's interpretation is incorrectly applied, which in turn has misled others. For example, in Sam Gill's introduction to Native American religions (1982:67), we find in reference to the Sacred Pipe: " . . . spiritual transfer that occurred as a result of long hours of concentrated smoking of strong tobacco." However, in Sacred Pipe ritual, the pipe is offered stem first to the spirits, and then circulated among the ritual participants until the tobacco is exhausted (nor do the Native tobacco mixtures in northern North America have hallucinogenic properties). If Brasser's theory of self-directed imagery were to be applicable, we would expect effigies to face the smoker under the conditions of the ritual; i.e., the effigy would be oriented away from the stem, so that it faced the smoker when offered stem forward in prayer. Brasser's theory is verified by the data. In all the premodern effigy-bearing Sacred Pipes with a ritual context, the effigies are oriented away from the stem (with the exception of several problematic pipes collected by Skinner [1926] from the Iowa. See Appendixes).

In a major exhibition of prehistoric artifacts of the Eastern woodlands and the Mississippi Basin (Brose, Brown, and Penny 1985), all effigies on one-piece pipes faced the smoker, while those requiring a separate stem were oriented in the opposite direction. Ewers (1986:47–104) illustrates a number of "effigy" pipes which he attributes to manufacture for trade to Euro-Americans from the early nineteenth century to the present; the effigies on most are oriented towards the smoker. Two slight-projection elbow pipes with a bear in place of the flange, the first collected by Paul, Duke of Wurtenburg, (Linden-Museum) in the early 1820s and the second by Catlin in the early 1930s (University of Pennsylvania Museum), have the bear facing the smoker. A similar pipe in Catlin's painting of the Missouri, *He Who*

Kills the Osages, has the bear facing away from the smoker (Hassrick 1977:75). Therefore, it may be assumed that separate-stemmed pipes with effigies facing the smoker, all postcontact, were most likely made, at least originally, for Euro-Americans. An example of such manufacture is a bowl in the shape of flying eagle facing the stem made for James Bruce, Earl of Elgin, when he was the Governor General of Canada from 1847 to 1854 (Brasser 1987:121, fig.111).

Of course, every generalization has its possible exceptions; e.g., a slight-projection elbow pipe with double-tapered bowl and square rim that has a sculpted bear in lieu of the flange facing the smoker. It was found in the grave of a child at a Pawnee village site in Nebraska inhabited between 1775 and 1815 (Ewers 1986:fig.10). A less likely exception, an elbow pipe collected by Dorsey (1904:fig.23) from the Skidi Pawnee in 1900 (Field Museum) which he calls a "sacred pipe of peace or war" (?), has four figures carved around the bowl—two animals and a man and a woman *in late-nineteenth-century Western dress*—and a turtle on the stem facing the smoker (the stem now with the pipe is not the one illustrated by Dorsey). A unique anomaly among effigy pipes is an elbow pipe collected by La Flesche (1921:pl.17a) from the Wind Clan of the Osage in 1913 (Smithsonian Institution) with a face on the bottom of the pipe (the round stem has a suspended scalp lock).

Effigy Symbolism

Of the effigies on Sacred Pipes, the rarest and most difficult to interpret are those of humans. Only one has been found in a ritual context, a "Janus" (double-faced) figure on an Iowa pipe collected by Skinner (1926). A pipe in the Übersee Museum with a Native human head facing away from the stem has pewter inlay emphasizing the numbers four and six with a clear four directions representation at the top of the bowl, indicating probable ritual intention (fig. 20). (On the back of the head are inset a cartridge head and a brass tack, although this appears to have been done after the original manufacture.) However, most of the human effigies have Western features and no known or plausible ritual context, such as the bearded image collected from the Crow (fig. 13), and a pipe given by Joseph Brant, the Mohawk supporter of the British during the American Revolution, to a Euro-American. In the latter pipe (now in the Museum of the American

Indian), probably of Ojibwa manufacture with an English silver chain dated 1789, the seated figure wears a European wig.

A sculptured effigy pipe is to be found in a Winnebago ritual bundle, with inscribed four directions symbolism on the top (fig. 31). The representation appears to be that of a horse. However, when the above photograph was seen by a Native shaman, she assumed it to be that of a spirit. When she saw spirits, their faces and bodies had an elongated appearance. (Similarly, the design engraved on the side of the early Omaha pipe illustrated in figure 2 may be of a flying spirit.) This Winnebago pipe is unique and illustrates the far-flung trading networks of Native people, for both bowl and stem are carved from baby walrus tusk ivory that had come down from the Arctic.

The majority of animal effigies are of horses and bison, were made at Pipestone since 1860, face the smoker, and were for the tourist trade. Even some that face away from the smoker, such as the relatively common, flat, arched-neck horse pipes, were usually made for the tourist trade. Ewers (1986:64) documents the selling of human- and horse-head pipes to tourists in 1861. Pipes with a sculpted buffalo in place of the flange are a common tourist pipe currently made at Pipestone, although the earliest known version was collected by Joseph N. Nicollet around 1838. The bowl of this particular pipe is in the form of a Janus-type Euro-American head wearing a top hat. Ewers (1986:fig.25) also considers this pipe "made for sale to white collectors."

An unusual one-piece pipe that was part of a Crow ritual bundle is a sculpture of a bison (or possibly a bear) whose tail forms the stem, through which smoke is drawn into the mouth. (fig. 35). Horse hoof marks were later inscribed on a Crow straight pipe (fig. 33). Both the bison and the horse were of major economic significance on the Plains, and the former is a major Lakota spirit. Other animals found represented on Sacred Pipes, without established ritual contexts, include prairies dogs (fig. 18), which have religious significance (see Grinnell 1889: 113–114), and bighorn sheep (Ewers 1986:56).

One of the earliest effigies to appear on pipes is the beaver. A beaver with inlaid eyes and incisors is found on a Hopewell (ca. 200 B.C.E.-200 C.E.) monitor pipe (Brose, Brown, and Penney 1985:63, pl.48). The earliest ethnographic pipe I have encountered is of proto-keel shape from the Northeast, and is similar to precontact Sacred Pipes from the Midwest with a "water monster" panther effigy. This pipe has a sculptured beaver rising above the bowl on the stem end facing away from the stem (fig. 44). Inscribed on one side of the bowl are a beaver, a flintlock, a saber, and a tomahawk, with a canoe with spirit figures, a female moose, and bow and arrows on the other side. On the front is inscribed a Christian cross, different from the Four Directions cross in that the lower line is longer than the others. The pipe is fascinating in its symbolism, indicating the precontact setting on one side and the beaver with postcontact trade items on the other. With contact and the fur trade, the beaver became of primary economic significance. In the Northeast, a purely Native Christianity spread among the Abnaki and Micmac in the seventeenth century (Bailey 1969:147); the pipe appears to be a Christian beaver effigy pipe of approximately the appropriate date. The decor of a keel bowl, probably Abnaki, in the Peabody Museum includes six beaver tails inscribed around the bowl.

A raised beaver is also carved in relief on the side of a Piegan straight pipe bowl, with an inscribed lizard on the other side (fig. 3). Here, Beaver is probably of other than economic significance. In Pawnee myth as in Blackfoot, Beaver has healing power (Grinnell 1889:109).

Another common effigy is of Bear, who is the major spirit of healing. Coming from Earth in the spring with new life, her cubs, Bear represents the healing and regenerative powers of Earth, of female energy. She is found sculptured on a Northeast keel pipe with tomahawk-shaped keel (fig. 47), and her head is on the projection of Cherokee (Linden-Museum) and Seminole (Peabody Museum) elbow pipes, as well as an eighteenth-century-Alabama long-projection elbow pipe (Fundaburk and Foreman 1957:pl.106). This mode of placing an animal on a pipe has been found among precontact pipes, like the catlinite pipe found in a Nebraska Phase site, dated to between 1175 and 1450 (Ewers 1986:fig.6).

As discussed in Chapter 3, Thunderbird is a major spirit in Sacred Pipe mythology. A keel pipe bowl, probably of Blackfoot or related culture, with four holes, has the Thunderbird inscribed on one side of the projection, with lightning inscribed on the other side (fig. 5).

An elbow pipe collected during the American Revolution by a British officer has inscribed on each of the two sides a snake and a bird. On the front is either an elk or a deer (fig. 45). All three animals exhibit zigzag spiritual power lines with forked ends coming from their mouths, a symbol motif used by the Ojibwa and related cultures. In the West, Elk is a spirit used in love medicine, but this interpretation here is unlikely. In a Pawnee myth (Grinnell 1889:105), Elk brings a human to the spirit world. Since birds and snakes also symbolize movement from the human realm to the spirit realm, for this pipe the more likely meaning of Elk is that of a spirit helper for shamanic travel.

STEM SYMBOLISM

The Stem

The symbolic significance of the stem is multiple. When married to the bowl for ritual use it symbolizes male energy and creative potential. As the channel for the smoke offering, the stem represents our voice and, as in Pawnee culture, may be decorated with black circular lines along the entire stem, making the stem symbolic of the trachea. The stem also represents the journey of life, which may be symbolized by a red line along the top of the stem. Representing life itself, the stem may be rubbed with red ochre mixed with bear grease, each symbolic of life-giving forces.

Shafts similar to stems, often without a smoke channel, are used in elaborate dance rituals (see Fenton 1953). These wands are ornately decorated, invariably with eagle feathers. The use of these wands in a particular widespread ritual has led to a misunderstanding that only the stem is important to the Sacred Pipe. However, the vast majority of pipes found in ritual bundles are unadorned, except, in a number of examples, for having been rubbed with red ochre. In some bundles, Pawnee for example, the pipe bowls are on the inside of the bundle, with the stems tied to the outside. Since pipe stems, being made of wood, will eventually become charred near the bowl end, undoubtedly they were replaced as required, while broken stone pipe bowls were repaired with lead.

Nevertheless, depending on ritual and individual spiritual inspiration, there are decorated pipe stems, exhibiting a rich symbolic world. These symbols can be discussed under the headings of carvings, coverings, and pendants.

Carvings

Except for intricate decorative piercing and cutouts or simple repeated incised lines, there are relatively few carved pipe stems. One unusual example in the Smithsonian Institution (Ewers 1986:pl.13) has a full human figure carved at one end of the stem (fig. 49). This stem probably belonged to the Cheyenne, Tall Bull, chief of the warrior Dog

Soldier Society (the museum listing has "Tall Chief"), and was most likely found by the United States Army after its attack on his camp at Summit Springs, 11 July 1869, when Tall Bull was killed (Berthrong 1963:342). Since the stem has four eagle feathers and scalp locks tied to the waist of the carved figure, it is clearly a stem for ritual use. Another example is an elaborately carved Menomini pipe stem, with the lightning symbol inscribed on one side and a turtle, the spirit of the shaking-tent ritual, incised on the other (fig. 43). The pipe was made following the maker's vision. In both cases, the significance of the carving, inspired by a personal vision, was probably known only to the maker.

Coverings

The simplest covering, aside from an ochre-bear grease mixture, is paint. A Menomini pipe from a war bundle (fig. 19) has a half-twisted stem painted blue, green, red, and yellow, the colors representing the four directions, which vary from one culture to another. Another relatively common application to the stem is brass tacks in double sets, usually of four or eight.

The most common decorative covering is quillwork. Except for the colors, the quills themselves are of no known symbolic significance (except see Chapter 3), although they may have symbolic patterns on ritual pipes, such as the footprints of buffalo or elk. Of significance are the birds' heads and feathers wrapped around some stems. Common are the duck, which may symbolize the re-creation of the world after the deluge, the horned owl, discussed in Chapter 3, and the red scalp of the female ivory-billed woodpecker. The bill of the latter is bent over backwards, according to the Iowa and other neighboring people, "in order to hold down the crest, for these birds erect their topknots when angry, and this is a peace pipe, and hence removed from wrath of all kinds" (Skinner 1926:224). A few pipe stems are wrapped with fur, probably of significance to the individual who made the stem or to the particular bundle of which it is a part (fig. 42).

Sweetgrass, usually in a braid, symbolizing the hair of the Earth Mother, or sage, two of the major purifying herbs, are at times tied to pipe stems or bowls when in not in use to preserve or increase their power (fig. 23). These purifying agents are functional rather than decorative.

Pendants

The most common addition to hang from a pipe stem are feathers, particularly those of the golden eagle, usually in a set of four, seven, or eight (fig. 1). Eagle has varying symbolic functions that differ from culture to culture, but in all cases is a major spirit. Eagle may represent Sun or West Wind. Eagle also represents the sending of our messages to the spirits, a meaning related to the trachea decor. The eagle feather may have eagle down appended to it and may be decorated along the shaft with quillwork. The pendant feathers may hang separately or be arranged in the fashion of a spread fan. In the East, turkey feathers shared some of the symbolism of Eagle, and in the Southeast flamingo feathers were used. Owl feathers were also hung from pipestems in a number of cultures, before the Christian impact made all female theriomorphic spirits a symbol of evil.

Also common are ribbons of varying colors that signify the Four Directions and particular spirits. The ribbons may be changed from ceremony to ceremony to indicate differing symbolisms. Horsehair, often dyed, usually red, is a frequent addition to stems. Red horsehair, stroud, feathers, and tassels are often linked to "the sun or sun's glow on the clouds at sunset" (Voget:73). War pipes may have pieces of scalps or scalp locks tied to the stems (fig. 15). A Northwest pipe (Peabody Museum) has two rattlesnake rattles along with eagle down suspended from the bowl rather than the stem.

Most pipes of the far Northeast have a beaded strip connecting bowl and stem, the beaded design most likely derived from dreams and visions (fig. 25). Frank Speck (1935:225) has written of these connecting strips, that they "are an illustration of the mantu' power in beads reinforcing the power of the act of smoking."

The possibilities of bowl and stem decorations are considerable, influenced not only by cultural variations, but also by individual vision experiences. Hence, the above discussion is but suggestive of the rich symbolic world of Native American religion.

V

Geography and History

DISTRIBUTION

Lack of comprehensive study has led to a number of inaccurate and misleading conventions in regard to the pipe. The keel shape is generally called "Micmac," although the first depiction is probably in a drawing by Linstrom in 1653 of a Delaware (King 1982:68); it is definitely depicted in a sketch of an Illinois by Nicolas around 1670. Its range extends throughout the northern half of the Sacred Pipe use area of North America. The T shape is usually called "Sioux," although its earliest depiction is with a Plains Cree (McDermott 1967:13), and the shape can be traced as far back as an Oneota example (see below). The elbow pipe without a projection is often understood as a pipe only used by females, an assumption contradicted by the evidence (see Appendix II). Finally, it is a common understanding that red stone (catlinite) is the preferred material. However, among pre-twentieth-century pipes, black pipes are as common as red, even among cultures that resided in the vicinity of known catlinite quarries. Black pipes, being less photogenic, are not illustrated as frequently as they are found in ethnographic collections.

In Chapter 2, it was pointed out that in the ethnohistoric sources, Sacred Pipe ritual was noted on contact with Native Americans by Europeans and Euro-Americans as early as the beginning of the seventeenth century, from the Gulf of the St. Lawrence to eastern New Mexico and from the lower Mississippi River to the Rocky Mountains. An analysis of separate-stemmed pipes found in the major ethnographic collections and illustrated in reliable early paintings indicates an even greater range. In the following section, the geographic range of the Sacred Pipe will be discussed according to the major pipe shapes (summarized in Map 1). The data from the mid-Atlantic must be understood as skewed, as most of the Native people there died from disease or were killed by Europeans early in the contact period. Since this region was extensively inhabited and farmed by Europeans long before collections of Native artifacts developed, one cannot assume that the present lack of artifacts indicates lack of use of the Sacred Pipe.

Elbow

The elbow pipe, including variations to frontal projections, has an extensive range covering most of North America below the Arctic. Examples can be found in the East from Maine to Florida, westward along the Gulf Coast to Louisiana, then northwestward through Oklahoma, Colorado, Utah, and eastern Oregon, then northward through Washington and central British Columbia into the Northwest Territories, then southeastward through the Canadian provinces to Quebec and back to Maine, and in all the land so circumscribed.

The Dogrib (Northwest Territories) example is problematic, for there is no ethnographic data accompanying it to indicate ritual use. Alexander Mackenzie claimed to have introduced the use of tobacco to the Slave and Dogrib Indians in 1789 (McGuire:422). The Dogrib pipe collected in 1868 and now in the Smithsonian collection has symbolic decor emphasizing the number four, but may have been brought from the south by Native traders.

Separate-stemmed pipes, however, are associated with the earliest semipermanent contact at James Bay. At the Fort Albany site, which would be no later than 1686, three pipes were excavated: an unfinished slight-projection elbow pipe of sandstone, the stemward part of a catlinite pipe with a small flange (similar to fig. 58), and part of an early form of the keel-shape pipe of limestone (Kenyon:pl.14) The northernmost examples with probable or certain ritual use would be from central British Columbia and northern Alberta and Saskatchewan.

Although the Southeast is not a separate-stemmed pipe culture area, there is an Apache pipe with little data in the Field Museum and

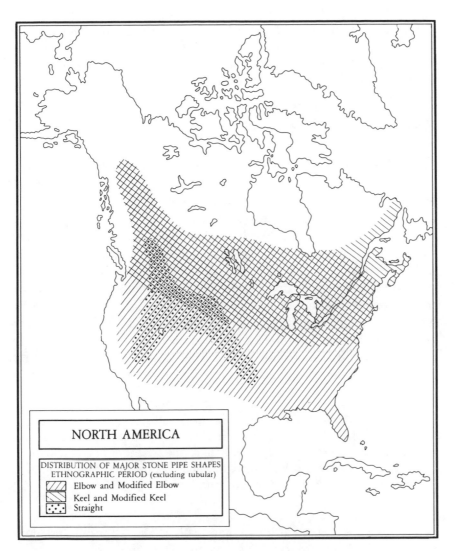

Distribution of Basic Sacred Pipe Shapes—Ethnographic Period

the previously discussed T-shaped pipe brought by the Sioux to the Navajo. If these two examples are included, the range of the elbow-shaped Sacred Pipe would include all of sub-Arctic Canada and the United States except for the Pacific coast.

Keel

The range of the keel shape overlaps the northern half of the elbow-shape range. Examples extend from Delaware through Pennsylvania and the northern midwestern states, and northwestward through Nebraska, the Dakotas, Montana, and into central British Columbia, then northwards into the Northwest Territory, then southeastward to the lower part of James Bay, then across Quebec and northeastward to the southern part of Labrador, and all through the land within.

The Northwest Territory keel-shaped examples, just as the elbow-shaped ones, have no accompanying data on ritual use. For the far Northeast, Frank Speck (1935:225) is often cited, without consideration of his reasons, on the lack of precontact ritual use of the pipe by the Naskapi and Montagnais. Speck's brief statement is quoted here as an example of how misunderstandings spread:

> That the smoking of tobacco is an instrumentality of magic [sic] among the Montagnais-Nascapi is apparent from several sources. And yet tobacco smoking has come into their life only since the advent of Europeans into the north. No tobacco was raised by them nor was the fashioning of stone pipes possible without metal tools.

Tobacco was raised at least as far north as Massachusetts and along the upper St. Lawrence River. Neither area is far from the Montagnais-Naskapi, considering the extensive precontact trade networks. Furthermore, Native people have a number of nondomestic smoking substitutes where tobacco is not available (see Chapter 1). More telling is Speck's second reason, which is similar to McGuire's earlier theory positing all but crude tubular pipes as European developments. This essentially racist viewpoint ignores an archaeological record replete with several thousand years of Native manufacture of highly refined stone artifacts without the necessity of European technology.

Straight

The straight shape is peculiar to the West. Examples can be found in Alberta, Idaho, Montana, South Dakota, Oklahoma, and Nevada. Several of the cultures that use the shape, such as the Cheyenne, the Lakota, and the Shoshone, consider it especially venerable and also use tubular bone pipes. For the Paiute and Paviotso in Nevada, straight pipes are the only available examples of the Sacred Pipe.

Circular and Disc

There are very few examples of the circular shape; those with a known provenance are from Oregon and Wyoming. However, Maximillian, Prince zu Wied, obtained one related to the elbow- with-projection shape along the upper Missouri in the early 1830s, and similar ones have been found in Wisconsin.

The disc pipe will be discussed primarily in the part of this chapter concerning archaeology, since it is an archaic shape. However, the Iowa and the Osage continued its ritual use. The examples were collected from the Osage after the establishment of reservations in Oklahoma. West's (1934:212–216) view that the sacred bundles in which these large pipes with the double triangle decor on the projection are found were war bundles is not confirmed by the available ethnographic data, although the interpretation is possible.

PAN-INDIAN IMPLICATIONS

Because the range of Sacred Pipe ritual and of the ritual artifact, in its diverse forms, includes most of the continent as well as a majority of the Native American cultures of North America, the conclusion is inescapable that the ritual complex is not distinctive of one or even a set of cultures, whether linguistically or ecologically related. Examples of the separate-stemmed pipe in museum collections or illustrated in early paintings were found for seventy-four distinct cultures or subcultures (see Appendix II), and this does not include much of the mid-Atlantic and Southeast, although it is certain from the enthnohistorical data that the Sacred Pipe was used there. If the ethnohistorical data were included, the number of cultures and subcultures would total over one hundred. In some areas, such as the Southwest, its use is limited to intertribal ceremonies with the cultures further north. However, for a large number of Native traditions, the Sacred Pipe is central to intratribal as well as intertribal religious practices.

An analysis of pipe bowl shapes from the ethnographic data with ritual associations demonstrates that no culture limited itself to a single shape for ritual use. Of pipes in the data base with ritual associations, seventeen cultures were represented by more than two examples. In all such cases, more than one shape was used (see table 1). (Figure 48 illustrates two unfinished pipe bowls, one keel and one elbow, by the same Ojibwa craftsperson.) The geographic spread for each shape is considerable, except for the straight bowl, which nevertheless is found in a large part of the West.

Since no pipe bowl shape is particular to a single culture, and since the Native cultures utilized more than one shape in the ritual of the Sacred Pipe, it is clear that the pipe bowl shapes are pan-Indian. Hence, what is essential to the Sacred Pipe is not the shape of the bowl, but the fact of its separate long stem. Because these findings on the ritual artifact coincide with the ritual itself, one can but conclude that the Sacred Pipe and its rituals have been a widespread pan-Indian religious complex in North America since well before the European penetration of the Americas.

THE PAST

The widespread ritual use of the Sacred Pipe combined with the fact that pipe styles are culturally nonspecific argues for a pan-Indian ritual complex over a large part of North America at the time of contact. The age of this religious complex remains to be discussed.

In all living traditions, innovation is continuous, yet there will be sufficient conservative aspects for cultural continuity. In parts of the Americas, such as the coast of Ecuador and Peru, a continuous ceramic tradition of over four thousand years illustrates considerable stylistic conservatism. In other areas, the time depths of traditions are less apparent but still present. In North America, the smoking complex is of considerable antiquity.

At Mummy Cave in northeastern Wyoming, a number of occupation levels have been delineated, the earliest being prior to 9000

Table 1
Distribution of Ethnographic Sacred Pipe Bowl Shapes
with Ritual Associations by Culture.

Culture	No. of Pipes	Disc	Elbow	Elbow pointed-proj.	Elbow slight-proj.	Keel	T*	Straight
Assiniboine	4		1		2	1		
Blackfoot	9		3		2	1	2	1
Blood	7				1	5		1
Cheyenne	5			1	1			3
Cree, Plains	7		1		2	1	3	
Crow	7		1		2		4	
Fox, Sauk	5			2	3			
Iowa**	9	1	5		2		1	
Mandan	5		1		4			
Menomini	6		1	1	2		2	
Ojibwa	4		2	2				
Omaha	4		2	1	1			
Osage	5	2			3			
Pawnee	11		2	3	3		3	
Peigan	9				1	4		4
Sioux***	11		2	3	5			1
Winnebago	4			1	2	1		
TOTAL	112	3	21	14	36	13	11	14

* Earliest example in listing ca. 1900. Other shapes have earlier dates.
** Plus one double-bowl elbow
***Plus one long-projection elbow and one effigy

B.P.(before present). Among the artifacts from approximately 4400 B.P. are tubular bone pipes (Frison 1978), which continue to be ritually used in the present by several Plains cultures.

Similar early dates are understood for tubular pipes in other areas of North America. Stone pipes appear around 4000 B.P. in Archaic sites in Illinois and 3000 B.P. on the Columbia River in Washington. Dated to approximately the same time are tubular pipes from the Sacramento area of California. The Glacial Kame culture of Indiana, Ohio, Michigan, and southern Ontario of this period evidences stone tubular pipes in the context of long distance trade (Fiedel 1987).

At some time in the more than four-thousand-year history of pipe smoking in North America, the Sacred Pipe with its attendant rituals and symbolism developed. The ritual of the Sacred Pipe has been discussed as a postcontact phenomenon, spread largely by Euro-Americans among Native cultures (see Fenton). More recently, Turnbaugh has argued that the ritual of the Sacred Pipe is to be understood as a postcontact nativistic movement (1977, 1979, 1980). This view has been countered by Blakeslee, but he, like Springer, continues to see pipe ritual as spreading into eastern North America in the postcontact period. These studies were based on ethnohistorical sources without comprehensive reference to artifacts and early illustrations. The earliest ethnohistorical evidence for the separate-stemmed pipe is in a drawing, published in Frankfurt in 1591, of a Native in "Florida" smoking a long-stemmed elbow pipe with slight projection (McGuire 1899:415, fig.45). Clearly, the Sacred Pipe was used in the East at the time of earliest contact.

On the other hand, Hall (1977, 1983) has made suggestions linking both round- and flat-stemmed Sacred Pipes to spear throwers and cross-cultural rituals, including the suggestion that some Hopewellian (200 B.C.E.-200 C.E.) "monitor" (platform) pipes had a wooden stem. His arguments are brilliantly imaginative but not conclusive. As discussed in Chapter 4, in general accord with the theory of self-directed design, Sacred Pipes with effigies and known ritual use almost invariably have the image facing away from the stem, that is, facing the smoker when the stem is pointed in the direction of the offering. On one-piece pipes, the effigies face the stem, as they do on Iroquoian ceramic pipes. Monitor effigies face the stem, while the effigies pipes of the Middle Woodland Period (C.E. 100–600), whose large stem bores indicate use of a separate stem, do not. Hence, the monitor pipes probably did not use a separate stem, as is also indicated by their small stem bores.

Although monitor pipes (fig. 49) of the Hopewell period are not separate-stemmed pipes, the widespread cultural influence and far-flung trade network of the period are evident in the presence of obsidian from western Wyoming, shells from Florida, copper from the shores of

Lake Superior, and chalcedony from North Dakota (Fiedel) in Ohio Hopewell sites. The superbly crafted monitor pipes have been found from the Missouri Basin eastward to the Atlantic as far north as Maine (see map 2). Rather than considering Hopewellian culture a single culture as in the past, archaeologists now conclude:

> These items and the ritual roles which can be posited for them serve to identify the cultural ties between the Ohio Hopewell and a series of distinct social groups spread across the continent. This system of cultural contacts has been called the Hopewell Interaction Sphere. . . . (Brose 1985:67)

Like the slightly later separate-stemmed pipe, the monitor pipe may well have served the same role as the Sacred Pipe in intertribal rituals. In any case, this pipe is the first clear example of a widespread pan-Indian specific and distinct pipe shape and concept. It should be noted that the distribution of the monitor pipe, although not a separate-stemmed pipe, coincides with the range of the ethnographic Sacred Pipe, except for extensions to the west and north. The pan-Indian pipe may have spread westward to the Rocky Mountains with the adaptation to the horse as some Missouri Basin and upper Mississippi Basin peoples moved further west, and the Sacred Pipe may possibly have spread northwards along the McKenzie River with the fur trade.

Indicating historical continuity is the direct stylistic relationship between the monitor pipe and the Sacred Pipe. There are several examples of rounded bowls on monitor pipes similar to those on late Mississippian elbow pipes. More explicit in indicating continuity is a monitor pipe with a specific diagnostic feature — double tapered bowl with rim — excavated in Iowa (New Galena site, Burial 1, Mound 23, 13ae5; Wedel 1959:fig. 4g) which is identical to bowls on precontact elbow pipes (fig. 12).

Blakeslee has traced the "calumet" to catlinite elbow-with-projection bowls from eastern Nebraska, dated to around 700 B.P. The earliest separate-stemmed pipe published, an elbow found at the Copena Site (Alabama), dated around C.E. 100–500 (Walthall 1980:122), would considerably predate the Nebraska finds. The latter date is approximately the upper limit for the Hopewellian monitor shape.

By the early Mississippian Period (ca. 900–1300), separate-stemmed pipes are well represented among extant cultural artifacts. At least one has continued in ritual use into the nineteenth century. At the Treaty of Dancing Rabbit Creek (1830), when the Choctaw were forced to give up their lands east of the Mississippi for land west of the river (Gaines 1928), a Mississippian type of effigy pipe (with head facing away from the stem) now in the Gilcrease Institute was ritually smoked.

The above discussion of the antiquity of the Sacred Pipe mentioned has ignored the importance of the disc shape. The disc pipe, usually dated from the thirteenth through the sixteenth centuries, is found widely distributed throughout north-central North America, including the upper Mississippi, Missouri, and Ohio, as well as the Lower Great Lakes drainage areas (see map 2). Its use continued in the ethnographic period among the Iowa and the Osage (fig. 29), where the pipe will be found in ritual bundle complexes given up in the early twentieth century. The disc pipe provides a direct connection between the Sacred Pipes of the ethnographic and archaeologic periods.

Elbow Sacred Pipes of similar antiquity are found in Omaha ritual bundles now in the Peabody Museum. The pipe illustrated in figure 2, used in hunting ritual, is similar to archaic pipes dating between the fourteenth and sixteenth centuries. The two pipes in the Sacred Tent of War Bundle (fig. 53) date by style to the seventeenth century, probably prior to contact for the Omaha.

Therefore, the Sacred Pipe as a pan-Indian ritual artifact could very conservatively be dated to the thirteenth century with the spread of the disc pipe shape, is more likely to be as early as the use of separate-stemmed pipes (at least sixth century), and is related to the monitor pipe of the Hopewellian period. The widespread use of the monitor shape indicates a pan-Indian ritual of tobacco smoke offering by the end of the second century B.C.E. Hence, pan-Indian pipe ritual is over two millennia in age.

The Straight Bowl

In Plains cultures, tubular pipes of hollow bone wrapped with rawhide, tanned leather, or fur continued in ritual use into the twentieth century. In this same culture area, straight pipes are among the most sacred of pipes. Since a straight pipe bowl is more awkward to use than an

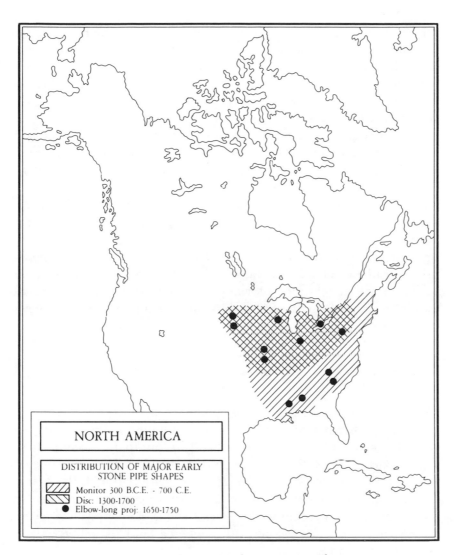

Distribution of Major Early Stone Pipe Shapes

elbow, we have the continuation of a sacred ritual implement of considerable antiquity modified by the ideology of the separate-stemmed pipe. Because there is no functional necessity to add a stem to the tubular pipe and as the tubular pipe continued in its own right, one can but assume that the potent symbolism of the separate stem was understood to enhance the sacredness of the pipe.

This evolution can be seen taking place in a precontact find from the Ramsey Mound in North Dakota (Montgomery 1906). Among several long catlinite tubular pipes from the find in the Royal Ontario Museum (e.g., HK938), there are several shorter than the others with a stem bore too wide for comfortable use in the mouth but wide enough for insertion of a stem (HK940). Similar pipes have been excavated in Manitoba (ROM: HK805) and Saskatchewan (HK 881). These pipes, approximately the same length as the ethnographic straight pipe bowls, are the earliest examples of the straight-shaped Sacred Pipe. The evolution of the straight pipe provides further evidence that the symbolism inherent in the separation of bowl and stem is of considerable significance.

The Modern Pipe

One factor that has led some anthropologists to discount contemporary pan-Indian religion is that the apparently recent modern shape is assumed to be Euro-American inspired. By a logic difficult to understand, therefore, modern pipe-centered religion is unauthentic. The most frequently encountered bowl shape since the late nineteenth century is the T, usually of constant thickness throughout, with a long, straight bore and stem that indicates drilling with a steel drill bit. Earlier pipes of related shape had a shorter projection with a tapered bowl, as well as tapered bore and stem holes.

The earliest datable T-shaped bowl is in an 1851 drawing by the Swiss artist Rudolph Kurz, done while he was at Fort Union on the Upper Missouri (McDermott 1967:11). Kurz decorated the pipe himself and gave it to a Cree chief, who ceremonially smoked it in the resident trader's office (Kurz 1937:203). The bowl was probably not of Native manufacture, for three months later Kurz (1937:257) was excited about buying a Native-made pipe bowl. Two years earlier, William G. Johnson, a traveler, noticed at James Bridger's trading fort "Some long, red stone pipes [roughed-out pipe blanks?] of St. Peter's Rock, from the upper Mississippi . . . are sold at $5; Mr. Bridger informed me there is a ready sale for them" (Alter 1962:234). Kurz probably obtained the pipe blank or Euro-American-made pipe bowl, which had become a standard trade item, for the pipe he made at Fort Union, which was considerably closer to the Minnesota quarry than Fort Bridger. Kurz thought the Native pipe he later obtained was made by an Eastern Sioux.

The Übersee Museum contains a pipe (fig. 40) collected in the same year (1851) that belonged to the Eastern Sioux chief Little Crow. This pipe, an elbow with slight projection, has a slightly tapered bowl and straight bored holes suggesting that the T shape was not made by eastern Sioux at this time. The earliest datable extant T-shaped pipe I have come across is in the British Museum (King 1977:23) with the date "1860" and a buffalo etched in reverse on the stem end of the bowl—most likely an early tourist item made at Pipestone, Minnesota.

I am aware of only two T pipes in museum collections with assumed earlier dates. In the Etnografiska Museet there is a pipe (1954.38.5) with an incompatible stem (one that does not fit) that, if the data are correct, would be earlier than 1850. A pipe (V-E-278) from the Speyer collection in Germany, now in the Museum of Man (Hull, Quebec), would date to around 1830, if the data are correct. Since both pieces were obtained from dealers, the accuracy of the dating may be in question.

By the 1860s, catlinite pipes were mass produced from the Pipestone, Minnesota, quarry for trade to Native people. Holmes (1919:263) estimated that between 1864 and 1866 nearly 2000 pipes were manufactured by the Northwest Fur Company for such trade, and in the winter of 1864–1865, a freight hauler named Hubbell had 5,000 pipes manufactured (Corbett 1982:68). The T shape is easy to manufacture with drill presses and continues to be so made for ritual use by Native people (Powers 1982:26), suiting the uniform thickness of the sheets of layered catlinite that are extracted from the Pipestone, Minnesota, quarry. This shape flooded the market, rapidly becoming the most common shape in the late nineteenth century. This interpretation is bolstered by the fact that the Blackfoot were primarily reached by Hudson's Bay Company traders coming from the Northeast rather than the Southeast, and they are the one major Plains culture not to have widely adopted the T shape.

It should be noted that the trade in pipes between Euro-Americans and Native Americans was a two-way affair. Most of the early-nineteenth-century elaborately carved pipes of the Ojibwa and of the Pawnee collected or drawn by Catlin (see Ewers 1979) were probably made for sale to non-Natives (see Chapter 4). William Clark began to collect such pipes on becoming superintendent for the Western tribes, with his headquarters in St. Louis, in 1816. Few of Catlin's or Bodmer's portraits show a Native holding an elaborately carved pipe as his or her own, although many have elaborately decorated stems.

What led to the traders adopting the T shape, aside from convenience of manufacture as well as the ready acceptance by Native people? A prototype of the T shape with rounded bowl has been found in an Oneota ritual context (Burke burial site in northeastern Iowa) no later than 1650 (Wedel 1959:fig.11c). Dating from the late seventeenth century to the early eighteenth century is the long-projection elbow shape (see Chapter 4 for description). A dozen examples have been located, and this shape has a distribution contiguous with that for the much earlier monitor pipe (see map 2), which was also T-shaped. It is found as well in at least one Lakota sacred bundle still in ritual use (Thomas 1941:pl.II). (See Appendix II for descriptions of the pipes discussed above.)

The T-shaped pipe from this Lakota sacred bundle is reputedly the White Bison Calf Pipe of the Lakota, an assertion more recently denied by several Lakota elders. In any case, the pipe is probably older than the movement of the Lakota onto the Plains. It is interesting that Thomas estimated the pipe to be approximately 250 years old, based on the orally recorded succession of bundle keepers. This is the same age the appearance of the pipe would suggest.

The long-projection elbow shape can be seen to derive from the disc pipe with prow shaped projection (fig. 28), as well as the contemporaneous double-tapered and rounded pipe bowls with similar prow (Hamilton 1967:fig.7a, 8a). (Figure 2 illustrates a precontact pipe with typical slightly angled rounded bowl on a square base, with a slight flange for a thong to the stem, and a shortened prow of the type found on late Mississippian period pipes.) The traders may have had the long-projection elbow pipe shape (fig. 7) described to them but had not quite understood its actual appearance, never having seen it. The pipe they did devise was sufficiently similar to gain Native acceptance. In other words, although the standard T shape is relatively modern, it is based on a widely-distributed shape of considerable antiquity and religious significance.

CONCLUSIONS

It is commonly understood that there are many highly diverse tribal religions in the Americas with but a few commonalities in specific geographical areas; e.g., the prairies of North America or the Amazonian forest. As tribal religions, these religions are assumed to be dead or dying, replaced by the Christianity of the dominant Euro-American culture. Where there are intertribal commonalities due to other than geographical features, they are assumed to be due to postcontact conditions (e.g., the Plains sun dance following the adoption of the horse), especially after the imposition of reservations (e.g., the Native American Church). Partially due to these commonly held incorrect assumptions, only in the last decade has religious freedom been explicitly granted Native religions in the United States. In Canada, the new Bill of Rights is not ipso facto assumed to apply to Native religions, which have no legal existence.

The research related above began with a similar understanding, assuming that pan-Indian pipe-centered religion was a contemporary phenomenon. Its intention was to delineate this modern development's historical antecedents, for potential use in Canadian court cases to help establish the legitimacy, from a Euro-American perspective, of contemporary pan-Indian religion. Surprisingly, analysis of the research indicated that the modern Native American pipe ritual is a pan-Indian religious modality of considerable antiquity, as old or older than the dominant religion of the invading Europeans. From the standpoint of the dominant culture, this constituted the "discovery" of a hitherto unknown major religious complex in aboriginal North America. Of course, Native elders had this understanding, but most scholars in a literate culture are unable to appreciate the historical accuracy of oral traditions, and it is difficult to separate ancient concepts from recent modifications.

The means by which this pan-Indian religious complex was integrated into the tribal religions varied from one culture to another. For example, it was and is primarily intercultural in Iroquoian cultures but intra- as well as intercultural among eastern, north-central, and Plains cultures. Regardless of the differences in its integration, the ritual of the Sacred Pipe was and is the common religious ritual of pan-Indian situations throughout sub-Arctic North America. Therefore, Pan-Indian Religion can be defined as a religious complex in which Native Americans from two or more traditional cultures participate in the ritual of the Sacred Pipe. The recognition of this religious complex should have important and positive effects, both intellectual and legal, on the understanding of Native North American religions, past and present.

For example, contrary to the view that there was no general ideology in much of Native North America (Gill 1982:35), the widespread use of tobacco as the primary sacrificial offering, not to mention the early widespread specific ritual for offering it, in and of itself indicates a common ideological foundation. Concerning the Americas in general, Wilbert (1987:201–202) writes, "The extraordinary dynamic power of this aspect of diffusion is evident in the rather strikingly similar tobacco ideology of American Indians that coincides with the limits of tobacco diffusion in the New World." For early North America, Brose (1985:67), in referring to the period of the monitor pipe two thousand years ago, points out that the ritual of intergroup exchange must have been "widely perceived as carrying a powerful and commonly accepted ideological message concerning relationships between society and the natural and supernatural worlds." The ritual of the Sacred Pipe, at least six hundred and probably fifteen hundred years in age, requires a specific cosmological understanding that continues to the present. The four points on prowed disc pipes (fig. 28), as well as the presence of four-directions symbolism on a monitor pipe (fig. 50), indicate this understanding to be at least two millennia in age.

The fact that contemporary pan-Indian pipe ritual is in accord with ethnohistorical descriptions from the earliest records, as discussed in Chapter 2, allows us to assume that this ritual is as old as the Sacred Pipe. Contemporary symbolism, when comparison is possible, is equally old. For example, the cross within a circle, representing the four directions in relation to the journey of the sun and the seasons, is found in Mississippian cultures, from around 1000 to 1600 (see Brose, Brown, and Penny 1985:108, fig.15; 145, pl.105). Hence, one may assume that the contemporary cosmological and theological understanding surrounding the Sacred Pipe at the very least relates to earlier conceptions. The concluding sections of Chapter 2 and 3 presented a generalized description of the current as well as traditional ideology surrounding Sacred Pipe ritual. Since it logically corresponds to the ritual itself, it is probable that this general understanding is of equal antiquity.

VI

EPILOGUE

Persecution and Revitalization

RESERVATIONS AND SUBJUGATION

The effects of five centuries of contact with Europeans on the Native peoples of the Americas is sufficiently well known not to require detailed repetition (see Berkhofer, Bowden, Crosby, Deloria, Drinnon, Grant, Jacobs, Jennings). In short, the major effect was decimation. It is generally accepted that many millions, over ninety percent of the population, died from epidemic European diseases for which Native Americans had no immunity: smallpox, measles, and others. The survivors, who welcomed the strange newcomers, were repaid with massacre, enslavement, deceit and pillage.

In the arable parts of North America, the Native people were continually pushed westward from their fertile gardens by British colonists, often causing Native peoples to fight each other for the shrinking land. The final push was across the Mississippi to the territory of Oklahoma, then unwanted by Euro-Americans. In the North, the French developed the mutually desired fur trade, although its end result was to seriously erode traditional values in the relationships of family, clan, tribe, and spirits. After the British took Canada from the French, the familiar pattern of land loss and reservations developed there. In the Southwest, after a successful seventeenth-century revolt against the Spanish by the settled or Pueblo peoples, an accommodation was reached, ensuring a degree of religious and cultural autonomy.

The net effect was to force Native peoples, when they were not deliberately exterminated as they were in Newfoundland, onto ever-shrinking parcels of land, beginning in the original British colonies in the East and yet to end in British Columbia in the West. After destroying the traditional economies and resources, nearly exterminating the bison, and establishing the reservations, the Euro-American governments set out to destroy the Native peoples' self-worth and world view. For those left alive, a policy of cultural genocide was implemented.

By the late nineteenth century, this policy was to put control, either official or de facto, of the reservations into the hands of Christian missionaries. The United States Army and the Canadian federal and provincial police were permitted to maintain the missionaries' will with force. The two governments also passed measures outlawing the practice of Native religions and forcibly removed children from their parents. Sent to residential schools, where many died of disease, the children were shorn of their roots and self-esteem. The net effect has been generations of despair, poverty, alcoholism, and suicide. Survivors were and continue to be frequently incarcerated by a legal system that is still largely racist (a situation apparent, for example, in the present official inquiry into the Marshall case in Nova Scotia and in the recent acceptance of American Native leaders as political refugees by the Canadian government).

Of direct relevance to this study is that most of the Sacred Pipes and other sacred items in museum collections are there because of the above policies. In carrying out the research, I was constantly aware of the tragic circumstances which placed these precious ritual items in my hands. I could only continue the work with my goal constantly in mind, that greater awareness of the rich Native religious heritage will assist in ameliorating the current situation.

Manuscripts associated with some of the collections document the cultural destruction. As early as 1884, Frances La Flesche wrote that the Sacred Tent of War Bundle, now in the Peabody Museum (file 84–75), was obtained from the family of its hereditary keepers because no one was left to care for it. However, it was not until the early twentieth century that the effects of missionary control became widespread in North America.

Clark Wissler, in a letter of 9 July 1903 to Franz Boas sent from Browning, Montana, lamented the continuation of tradition: "Prices are high and the real 'medicine' is almost unobtainable at any price."

In the same year, William Jones wrote to Livingstone Farrand that the few remaining traditionalists would not sell old pipes, but Catholics would. At this time, the selling of sacred items to anthropologists was still considered cultural treason. In Wissler's letter to Farrand, dated 25 June 1904 from Browning, we find, "The fact the [sic] a crazy Indian killed seven out of a family that gave me some important medicines last year has made them cautious." (All of these and the following letters are in the archives of the American Museum of Natural History.)

By the next decade, the traditions had further deteriorated. There is documentation with an Hidatsa sacred skull bundle indicating that some Native people now saw the museums as the only appropriate repository for their religious heritage. A letter from Henry Wolf Chief, dated 18 January 1911 at Independence, North Dakota, describes the situation:

To whom it may concern:-

. . . I was about twelve years old when I first learned about these skulls and a man whose name was Missouri River was the keeper. Soon after this my father, Small Ankle, became the keeper of the skulls and kept them for fifty years. My father died in 1899 and after that I with my two brothers took care of the skulls.

I asked . . . to take the skulls to his place and keep them as he was one of the oldest members of the clan; but he refused because a long time ago the Government stopped the people from having ceremonies and shrines like that. "Let it stay there," he said, "and perhaps the house will fall down on it and cover it up. I don't want it."

I asked another member of the clan . . . to take it. I told him I did not believe in the shrine any more for I was a Christian. I asked him two different times but he did not want it at all. [Three other clan members are asked and refuse.]

These persons whom I asked to take the shrine believed in the old ways. I did not ask any of the younger men who were Christians to take it. Although they are members of this clan, they do not know the stories connected with such things and do not care about them.

So I tried to take care of it myself. I cleaned up around it and covered it up on rainy days. However as I did not believe in it any more I decided to bury it near my father's grave. At this time Mr. Wilson came to me . . . He wanted to buy it but I told him, no, "This was my father's and I am going to bury it near by his grave." I refused him about three times. I studied about what Mr. Wilson told me that it was a mistake to bury it. He said that they wanted to keep it in a good place better than it had ever been in before, and would keep it always. Then I decided to let Mr. Wilson have it.

When I had sold it . . . came to my house and I told him all about what I had sold to Mr. Wilson. He said, "That is all right, for you don't believe in those things and I don't either, for we are Christians. I am glad you sold it, for I was afraid that sometimes you might pray to it. You asked those persons to take it but they did not want it; so it was all right to let Mr. Wilson have it. I used to have such things myself but I do not have them any more." [The letter details rumblings about the sale in the community which stopped when the circumstances were understood.]

When I sold it I thought it was all right for me to sell it. Then I heard that they kept it in a good house in New York, and I was glad I sold it. I saw a picture of the house where they keep it; and it is a rock house and it will last for a long time. They also have all the stories about it to keep with it. I still believe what they told me; that they want to keep it in a good house and keep it forever. [The names of those mentioned as refusing to accept the pipe have been deleted.]

A second letter by one of those that Wolf Chief asked to take the bundle, repeats the circumstances and contains the following consent:

Again Wolf Chief came to me and said he was going to sell the skulls and I agreed for him to sell them. I said it was going to be better to sell them where they could be taken care of than to bury them, or even to leave them in the earth lodge which might fall on them and cover them up.

A half year later, Gilbert Wilson forwarded a Hidatsa pipe (fig. 8) to the American Museum of Natural History with letters and affidavits describing a circumstance where a traditionalist woman traded a flat pipe from her husband's Eagle Hunting sacred bundle for a tribal one, which someone else had sold Wilson. She also gave him $5.00 for the "difference in value"!

That same year, a major bundle was obtained from the Osage for the Brooklyn Museum. The collector, Stewart Cullin, documents the cultural atmosphere at that time (1911:33):

Mr. La Flesche tells me that the Osage are about through with their medicine bags, will have only one more ceremony, and then discard them forever. A young man at the dance house on Sunday said he had recommended that the tribe should collect all their old things and hand them over to the Government, to be kept in the National Museum or some similar depository. Mr. La Flesche explained to me that they are so divided that such a plan was impossible. They are anxious to sell them, and are only deterred by the fear that some harm will come to them if they let them go.

Culin poignantly describes the parting of the Osage bundle (fig. 29) he obtained from its keeper (1911:27):

> . . . a middle-age woman with a careworn face, who owned the bag. After some delay she produced it . . . I was informed she would sell it for $100. She laid the bag in my hands.. . without delay, I said would take it at her price. A period of suspense followed. The woman seemed to experience violent emotion. She held the bag in her arms and nursed it as if it was a child . . . At last, after a great effort she yielded.

ADAPTATION AND REVITALIZATION

European values and Christian priorities subtly influenced Native ideology soon after contact, although religious practices per se changed little. The impact of the hierarchical and patriarchal, if not misogynist, European culture on the mostly egalitarian (see Leacock 1978) and often matrilineal North American Native cultures led to a shift in the understanding of the other-than-human relations (Paper 1983:20). The generic term for spiritual powers in a number of Native languages came to be understood as a single male deity, Creator or Great Spirit, but the ritual of the Sacred Pipe maintained the precontact dual offering to the female Earth and male Sky. Adaptations of greater cultural consequence took place as Native leaders sought to counter Euro-American domination and revitalize their despondent people. Of the many developments, four examples will be presented, in historical order, leading to the contemporary one that emphasizes the Sacred Pipe.

The Longhouse Religion

Ganeodiyo (Handsome Lake), a Seneca, suffered from the common malaise of late-eighteenth-century Six Nations males, loss of function and corresponding loss of self-esteem, resulting in alcoholism and despair. Near death, he had a series of visions that led not only to a personal transformation, but to a revitalization of traditions, albeit with major changes, particularly in regard to the socioeconomic role of women and religious ideology (see Wallace 1969). Under Quaker influence, the shift was from large, clan, gynecocratic dwellings, with the gardening carried out by the women, to the European model of small, nuclear family, patriarchal cabins, with farming done by the men. Strong-willed women who objected were persecuted as witches.

On the other hand, traditional ceremonies were revived, and Ganeodiyo's followers developed a semi-institutional religion that has continued to the present among the Six Nations people. The traditional medicine societies, such as the False Faces, continued among the followers of the modified religion. The major change in religious ideology, as Tooker (1964:81) has suggested, is "that Haveniyu, 'Great Spirit' or 'Controller,' which Handsome Lake called the Creator, has been substituted for the older 'Sky' in Iroquoian religion by Handsome Lake: in present Iroquoian cosmology, the Creator occupies the place of Sky in early accounts."

It is among Mohawk followers of the Longhouse Religion at Akwesasne that one of the first modern demonstrations against the dominant culture's violation of treaties with Native peoples took place. In 1969, the border crossing between New York and Ontario on reserve land was blockaded over the plan of the Canadian government to take Mohawk land without permission. The protest was led by traditionalists and was influential in the development of the American Indian Movement, AIM (see below). Over the violent objections of assimilationists, the traditionalists at Akwesasne created their own school using their own language, and a newspaper (recently firebombed) with a worldwide circulation. Traditional religious practices and sociocultural roles, including the position of Clan Mother, were revitalized. This struggle continues today.

Cherokee

It is another Iroquoian-speaking people, the Cherokee of the Southeast, that have experienced both the greatest adoption by Native people of Euro-American culture, and the greatest failure of assimilation in changing the response of Euro-Americans to Native peoples. In the early eighteenth century, the Cherokee had adopted plantation farming, frame and brick Euro-American buildings, a syllabic written language, printing presses, newspapers, and a tax system. In 1827, they adopted a formal constitution with a bicameral legislature. Under this constitution, women in this matrilineal culture were disenfranchised (Hudson 1976:451). Missionaries were a major influence on these developments (Bowden 1981:174–175).

A primary motivation for the Cherokee in making major changes in their culture was to secure their land against the avaricious Euro-Americans. They assumed that if they completely acculturated they would be left alone. However, their considerable economic success, combined with the discovery of gold in Georgia, led to their shortly being forced, robbed of their possessions, at bayonet point on "The Trail of Tears" to Oklahoma in 1838. The heritage of the Trail of Tears was to turn Native reformers away from assimilation. In Oklahoma, the Trail's terminus, the Native American Church received its greatest impetus.

Native American Church

At the beginning of the reservation period in the Plains, a new religion, based on a synthesis of Mesoamerican religious practices and the Midwestern Medicine Lodge, spread northward. By the early twentieth century, the religion had spread into the Great Lakes area (see La Barre 1975). Subject to many interpretations, Christian content varied considerably. The version of John Rave that reached the Winnebago was Christian in all but acceptance by other Euro-American Christians. It was this version's intolerance of Native religious traditions that led to the "giving away" of sacred myths and sacred items to the anthropologist Radin, discussed in Chapters 2 and 3.

The adherents of this religion organized to incorporate on the model of Protestant churches. The first incorporation was in Oklahoma in 1914 as the "First-born Church of Christ." Eventually the name was changed to the "Native American Church," which incorporated in a number of states. Although legal acceptance has been difficult and spotty, the Native American Church was the first Native religion to be recognized by the United States, and peyote has recently become legal for Native religious use in Canada (Stewart:336). Recent estimates place the number of adherents at a quarter of a million, the majority of whom also participate in other forms of Native religion. As a pan-Indian mode of religiosity that emphasizes the direct experience of the numinous in a communal ritual context, the Native American Church is the first major Native religious adaptation to succeed in the postreservation context.

American Indian Movement

More traditional forms of Plains religion also underwent revitalization and adaptation to the changed circumstances in the reservation period. Beginning with the Shoshone at the turn of the century (see Jorgenson), a somewhat modified "Sun Dance" spread to the Bannocks, Utes, Crow, and Arapaho. Modifications continue among the Wind River Shoshone and Arapaho:

> . . . great attention paid to God as personal Creator and Father. Arapaho Offerings Lodge worshippers can be seen to wear scapulars, rosaries, and medals about their necks, and Christian symbols on their beaded aprons. Recent tradition says that each participant over the three-day period should dance to each one of the twelve side poles, which now represent the apostles in their positions around the Center, Christ. (Starkloff 1974:133)

While such adaptations to reservation conditions and Christian domination developed, more traditional practices went underground. Although Indian agents reported the demise of traditional religion on many reservations, it continued away from the settlements among a minority of Native peoples. The continuation of these traditions formed the core of a revitalization movement that has been growing exponentially over the last decade and a half.

In 1968, several Ojibwa, including Eddie Benton-Banai, Dennis Banks, and Clyde Bellecourt founded the American Indian Movement (AIM):

> Although much of its inspiration derived from Indian fishing-rights battles already underway in Washington and Oregon, from Six Nations ("Iroquois") land protests in Ontario and New York, and from the "Red Power" activity that had evolved out of civil-rights activism on the West Coast, AIM came into existence as a direct result of the termination and relocation programs that dumped thousands of bewildered Indians into the cities (Matthiessen 1983:37).

PLATE I *Tubular Pipes*

9. Catlinite tubular pipe, found in Wisconsin. Length 12.8cm. MPM 14027.

10. Cheyenne bone tubular pipes covered with ochre-rubbed rawhide or fur.　MAI 10/4494, 2/8363, 12/3093.

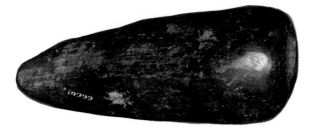

11. Clay (L) and stone (R) Hopi (Oraibi) ritual tubular pipes. FM 66601, 44066.

12. Pipe found in Wisconsin, late Mississippian type. Length 7.8cm. MPM 14101.

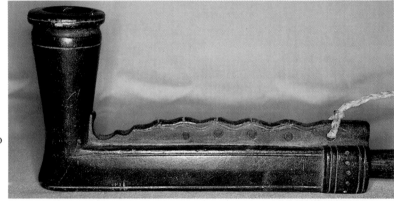

13. Pawnee pipe from Evening Star Bundle (kept wrapped in buffalo wool). AMNH 50.1/8421A [142].

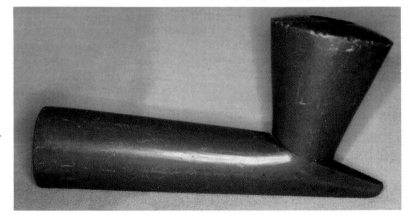

14. Elbow pipe with pointed projection owned by Black Hawk, ca. 1830. MPM 2761 [160].

PLATE III   *Elbow Pipes With Slight Projection*

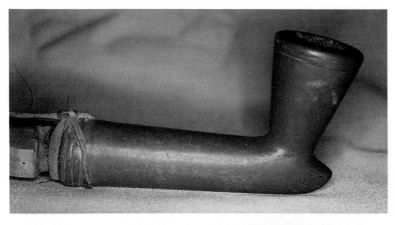

15. Osage pipe
with scalplock tied
to stem.
FM 71718 [123].

16. Pawnee pipe
from ritual bundle
with thong for
attachment to stem
during rituals.
FM 71872 [140].

17. Double-bowl
elbow pipe: Iowa
Thunder-Eagle gens
pipe (?), stem not
illustrated.
MPM 31492 [74].

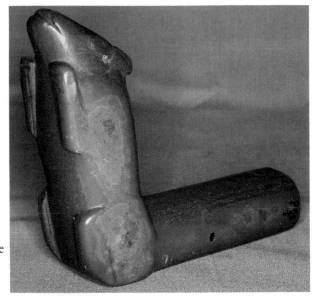

18. Plains prairie
dog effigy pipe.
AMNH 50/598.

19. Crow effigy
pipe.
MAI 2/4419.

20. Effigy pipe of
unknown origin
(end of projection
broken). UM 09172.

PLATE V   *Long-projection elbow and* T *Pipes*

21. Archaic pipe
found in Wiscon-
sin. Length 8.7 cm.
MPM 14250.

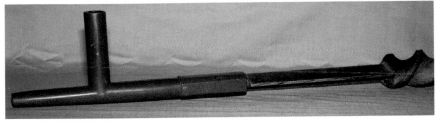

22. Menomini pipe
from war bundle.
AMNH 50.1/5853 [90].

23. Plains Cree rit-
ual pipe.
APM H80.5.4ab [48].

24. Pasamaquody pipebowl. AMNH 50.1/7771 [130].

25. Montagnais pipes from Labrador (upper) and Quebec. SI 90307, 90306, 395329 [See 100–101 for similar pipes.]

PLATE VII   *Keel and Disc Pipes*

26. Large Blood
pipe with complex
engraving and four
holes
FM 51632 [24].

27. Archaic pipe
found in Wiscon-
sin. Length 6.7 cm.
SMPM 14023.

28. Disc pipe
found in Wiscon-
sin. Length 8.1 cm.
MPM 14022.

29. Osage pipe
from ritual bundle.
BMA 06.64A [125].

PLATE IX   *Circular Pipes*

30. Arapaho pipe.
FM 61457 [4].

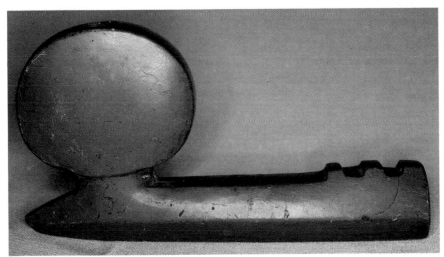

31. Pipe found in
Wisconsin. Length
12.0 cm.
MPM 14095.

32. Cheyenne Sun
Dance Pipe.
FM 96821 [34].

33. Crow pipe with
Dipper motif.
FM 69554 [54].

PLATE XI　　　　　　　*Unusual Effigy Pipes*

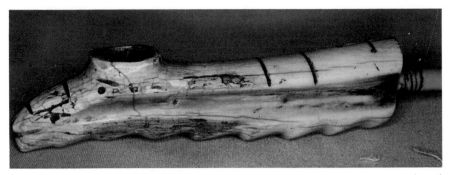

34. Winnebago
ivory effigy pipe
from ritual bundle.
FM 14901 [196].

35. Crow one-piece
effigy pipe from
ritual bundle.
MAI 21/545 [50].

36. Ojibwa pipe
bowl.
NMM III-G-825
[110].

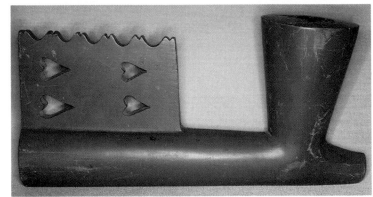

37. Iowa clan bun-
dle pipe.
MPM 30538 [75].

38. Ojibwa pipe
collected in 1813.
NMM III-G-1098
[107].

PLATE XIII

Inlaid Pipes

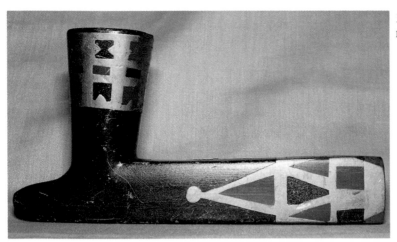

39. Arapaho pipe. LM 40283.

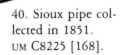

40. Sioux pipe collected in 1851. UM C8225 [168].

41. Detail of inlaid T-shaped pipe. MPM 20222.

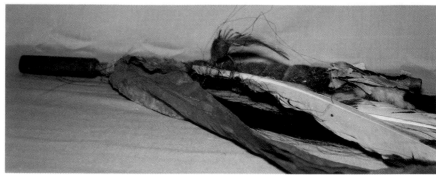

42. Blood "Beaver
Pipe."
AMNH 50/5413 [21].

43. Menomini rit-
ual pipe.
MPM 4447 [93].

44. Kaw pipe with
two stems: catlinite;
quillwork common
in the late nine-
teenth century.
MAI 2/7133.

PLATE XV   *Engraved and Sculpted Effigies on Pipes*

45. Pipe collected
in late eighteenth
century.
NMM V-E-300 [190].

46. Early
Pasamaquody pipe.
AMNH 50.1/9850
[132].

47. Pasamaquody
pipe.
AMNH 50.1/9849
[131].

48. Two unfinished bowls by same Ojibwa maker, ca. 1900.
NMM
III-G-311/310.

49. Hopwell "monitor" pipe found in Wisconsin.
MPM 13978.

50. Top of figure 49.

51. The two pipes in the Omaha Sacred Tent of War Bundle. (#119, #120; Chapter VI, p. 102].

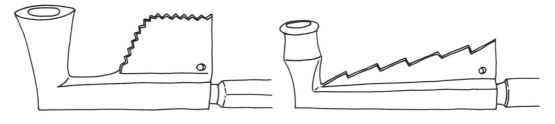

AIM began with social services, legal rights, community protection, and urban education programs in the Minneapolis-St. Paul area, but quickly attracted young Native people from all over North America.

By 1970, AIM also attracted traditionalist religious leaders, including the Lakota, Leonard Crow Dog, who was both a leader in the Native American Church and in the underground traditional ceremonies, including the nonmodified sun dance. Within a few years, the older traditionalist elders John Fire Lame Deer, Frank Fools Crow, Pete Catches, and Wallace Black Elk had become AIM spiritual advisers. Crow Dog and Black Elk were at the Second Battle of Wounded Knee throughout most of the confrontation, which was instigated by the request of Fools Crow, as spokesperson for the Oglala chiefs, for AIM's help (Matthiessen 1983). The young and the elderly had, in effect, formed a traditionalist-oriented coalition against the assimilationist middle-aged. In 1973, most of AIM's leaders attended their first sun dance, led by Lame Deer and Crow Dog. AIM was as much a religious movement as one of sociopolitical reform: at the heart of the movement was the sweat lodge and the Sacred Pipe.

Through all of these activities, the Sacred Pipe was the primary symbol of revitalized people and traditions. "On the 'Longest Walk' to Washington in the late 1970s [as in the Canadian walk to Ottawa in 1974] the Sacred Pipe was the religious symbol to unite many diverse tribes from all over the United States" (Steinmetz 1984:71). The Sacred Pipe, now as in the past, is the primary pan-Indian ritual.

Since that time, many young Natives have sought out the elders of their own traditions, and fasting is again becoming the means for youths to come to terms with themselves and all their relations:

> . . . the high school, where senior citizens had taken over a small room in the basement. A dozen of the old-timers spent their days making pipes. Large blocks of catlinite had been transported from Pipestone, Minnesota, and they used the school's power drill to make the holes in the bowls quickly. They sat around talking and smoking, filing away at the half-finished pipes. Rods of ash wood were stacked on one of the tables for the pipe stems. Business picked up in the springtime when young men would be going on vision quests or preparing for the sun dance, so they worked busily turning out the pipes in assembly-line style (Powers 1982:27).

Elders conferences have become increasingly popular on college campuses with Native students as well as in urban areas with Native populations. Gatherings of youths seeking the tutelage of traditional elders have taken place over much of North America. Describing a 1983 youths and elders conference held on the Oklahoma ranch of the Creek Indian, the late Phillip Deer, a spiritual leader of AIM, Vecsey (1984:203) writes, "Around the central fire a gathering of American Indians representing dozens of tribes from North, Central and South America is enacting the ceremony of the pipe. . . . " Many powwows have shifted their focus from dance competitions to a more traditional gathering, including sweat lodges. In all of these gatherings, the Sacred Pipe fulfills the need for a religious ceremony with which Natives from all traditions can identify.

Former AIM leaders have shifted their energies from political confrontation to education and religious revitalization. For example, Eddie Benton-Banai is the spiritual leader of the Three Fires Society, a revival of the Nishnabe (Ojibwa) Midewiwin (Medicine Lodge) tradition, that has spread from Wisconsin north to Manitoba and east to central Ontario. In areas where the traditions have virtually been lost, as in the eastern New England states and the Atlantic provinces of Canada, sweat lodges and Sacred Pipe rituals are again being practiced by a growing number of young Native people.

CHRISTIANITY AND RELIGIOUS FREEDOM

The Effects of Vatican II

Until recently, Christian missionaries in the main damned Native American religious understanding and practice, calling it the work of the devil. Converted Native people, whether or not by choice, were forbidden to participate in what was termed "sorcery" and "witchcraft." At the instigation of missionaries, Natives were jailed for participating or even speaking about traditional ceremonies. Even in the early 1970s, police, called in by missionaries, at times violently disbanded those attending rituals, and traditional healers were ostracized (Paper 1980).

Vatican II led to a radical shift in these attitudes, not only within Catholicism, but also within the liberal Protestant churches. The *1977 Statement of U.S. Catholic Bishops on American Indians* spoke of respect for the "distinctive traditions, customs, institutions and ways of life of its peoples" and that the "Gospel message must take root and grow within each culture and each community." In 1986, the United Church of Canada issued an apology to Native peoples for the means used in bringing Christianity to them.

Increasingly, some Catholic priests have incorporated elements of Native religions into the Mass and some Native priests, the Ojibwa Father John Hascall for example, function as both Catholic priest and traditionalist healer (Vecsey 1987). Younger Native Anglican priests and United Church ministers feel comfortable with the sweat lodge and the Pipe. For many of these ministers and priests, the Sacred Pipe is the symbol that conjoins the two traditions.

Even before the effects of Vatican II, Father Paul Steimetz, S.J., sought to use the Sacred Pipe to mediate between Christianity and Lakota traditional religion. As early as 1965, he prayed with the pipe and brought the pipe to the mass altar (Steinmetz 1980,1984).

This turnaround by the churches at first confused Native peoples. Many of the middle-aged generation were resentful at the contradiction: the Church first taught them to abhor traditional religious ways and then told them to embrace the old ways. However, a decade after the reversal, there has been a sudden growth in traditional practices, especially on reservations that had lost their past. For example, on southern Ontario Ojibwa reserves where fasting had not taken place for well over a half century, some youths are again fasting, and sweat lodges are becoming familiar sights.

"We Also Have a Religion" (spoken by Red Jacket in 1805)

The reversal by the Churches removed the pressure on the governments to force Christianity on Native peoples. This factor, combined with the awakening of political liberals to the cultural genocide and physical oppression of government actions, symbolized by the 1973 Battle of Wounded Knee, led to the passage of a Congressional resolution specifically legitimizing Native traditional religions: Public Law 95–341 – 11 August 1978. Although this resolution does not have the force of law and has had minimal impact (see Michaelsen 1982), it does symbolize a start towards freedom of religion for Native peoples in the United States.

In Canada, the laws prohibiting the practice of Native religions were de facto revoked with the revision of the Indian Act in 1951

(Patterson 1972), but religious freedom for Natives in Canada did not follow. Although the new Bill of Rights for the first time gives Canadians a written partial guarantee of religious freedom, the federal government has not been willing to state that it applies to Native religions (personal correspondence with Canadian cabinet ministers). Of the many religions accepted as legitimate by the federal and provincial governments, Native religions are conspicuously absent.

Enforcement officers have been even slower to recognize the changed understanding of the churches. For example, as recently as 1986 Canadian Customs and Immigration officers held a Native woman, without charge and under conditions that would be illegal if applied to animals, for carrying traditional red willow bark with her Sacred Pipe. Native people are still harassed by officials on both sides of the border for carrying sacred items, such as eagle feathers hung from a pipe stem, that are controlled by specific laws.

The 1978 Joint Resolution on American Indian Religious Freedom specifies "traditional religions." The courts have specifically not considered religions that can be determined "a twentieth century cult" to have the protection of law (State vs. Whittingham: Arizona Court of Appeals 1973).

In this regard, there is a common misunderstanding of the pan-Indian use of the Sacred Pipe as a modern phenomenon. Even those who have studied the Pipe and are personally involved in its religious use have mistaken its history. Steinmetz (1984: 71) has written, "I believe the Sacred Pipe is the first pan-Indian symbol since peyote united many tribes in the Native American Church." Other scholars have argued that basic pan-Indian theological concepts, e.g., the Earth as a female nurturing spirit, are due to Euro-American influence (Gill 1987). These inaccurate views bias the courts away from recognizing the legitimacy of pan-Indian religion, the major form of Native religion to be found in the many modern pan-Indian contexts: cities, schools, gatherings, and prisons. Yet it is in pan-Indian contexts that the Sacred Pipe has a ritual role of great antiquity. Will and Hyde (1917) have documented trade centered on corn in the Plains from the earliest ethnohistorical sources, and these same sources point to the Sacred Pipe as the mediating ritual.

Understanding religion from the Christian model, the dominant culture and authorities have difficulty in recognizing a religion without institutions, doctrines, sacred texts, or a history (based on a Western conception of time). This difficulty is compounded when the religion has no name or other formal characteristics.

Because Christianity has traditionally placed a primary value on belief, belief has become central to the Western understanding of religion. For example, the usual question of religious identification revolves around belief. However, in most of the world's religions, behavior is accorded more concern than belief. That the former is observable and the latter subjective and individual in nondoctrinal religions indicates behavior to be the more objective criterion for defining non-Christian religions. Hence, awareness of patterned religious behavior, that is, ritual, can lead to a recognition of contemporary pan-Indian religion.

Of the pan-Indian religion's two primary rituals, the sweat lodge is a circumpolar religious complex. However, the offering of tobacco smoke to sacred entities is particularly American, and the kind of pipe utilized in the pan-Indian pipe-centered religion has been specific to North America from the western mountains to the Atlantic Coast. In the previous chapters, it has been demonstrated that the history of the Sacred Pipe and of its ritual indicates that pipe-centered religion, rather than being a modern development, is a pan-Indian religious complex at least six hundred and probably over two thousand years of age, as old if not older than the religion of the dominant powers in the Americas. It is hoped that an understanding of this historical dimension will help the governments of Canada and the United States recognize pan-Indian Native American religion, cease persecuting it, and accord the Native religions of the Americas the same status it does to the religions of immigrants to the Americas.

THE CIRCLE

As this book was being written in the autumn of 1987, a unique gathering took place at an Anglican retreat center in central British Columbia. At the invitation of the Dialogue with People of Living Faiths subunit of the World Council of Churches, a small number of Native elders and spiritual leaders, together with the leaders of the councils of Native ministers of the Anglican and United Churches of Canada, met with a commissioner and a staff person from the World Council of Churches headquarters in Geneva. The meeting was intended to be a step in the direction of reversing a half-millennium of Christian persecution and suppression of Native spirituality. The Native representatives came from both coasts, from the far north and the southern United States, and from the center of this continent, Turtle Island.

After a sweat lodge ceremony, a circle gathered about four Sacred Pipes, representing the east, west and center, with a woman's pipe for the female spiritual energies. After an elder's helper prepared and filled the pipes, the four elders who were the keepers of the Sacred Pipes pointed the stems of their Pipes toward the spiritual powers and prayed to the spirits for their guidance and aid. The Pipes were lit and the verbal petitions accompanied by the smoke offering continued. The Pipes were then passed to the left to be relit, and then were repeatedly passed around the circle until the tobacco offering was completely smoked.

The circle was made up of Natives and non-Natives, traditionalists and Christians. All shared the Sacred Pipe and offered smoke. All in harmony offered their prayers with the same ritual, but in individual ways for the same goals: to end strife and bring peace to all the people, to end the suffering of the oppressed and persecuted, for the children to grow in dignity and wholesomeness, and for the end of the destruction of our mother, the Earth. As the Sacred Pipes went around the circle, the smoke from each flowed together and became one offering, and the people became one, voicing one prayer.

As in the past, so in the present, the Sacred Pipe serves as a means for people of different cultures and traditions to join together. To join in their innermost being, to together make a sacred offering and speak to those powers and persons who gave us life and whose continued presence gives meaning to that life.

Notes on Methodology

IDENTIFYING RELIGION THROUGH RITUAL ARTIFACTS

The study of prehistoric religions is difficult, because normal research methodologies are inapplicable. History of religions developed out of the comparison of religious texts. Archaeology can lead to understanding the material aspects of cultures, and by extension the socioeconomic aspects, but remains silent on ideology without the aid of texts or supplementary information. Ethnology obtains information from living cultures, but this data cannot ipso facto be applied to the past. Ethnohistory is dependent upon recorded observations and cannot push beyond the first contact with nonliterate cultures.

In studies of early Chinese religion (Paper 1978, 1986), I found it possible to gain some understanding of the religious ideology of the protohistoric period by focusing on the iconography of the central religious artifacts. I had available to me both the methods of comparative symbolism and knowledge of the functions of the religious artifacts and ideology from partial literary material slightly later in time.

For the precontact Native American religious traditions north of Mesoamerica, we do have religious artifacts and we do have early observations recorded by Europeans and Euro-Americans. To utilize the latter material, we must be aware of the source's cultural background and purpose, in order to discern observation from interpretation and assess the reliability of each. This is the approach I used in an earlier study of aspects of Native American religious ideology at the time of contact (Paper 1983).

In the present study, my task was somewhat different. I set out to understand the history of modern pan-Indian religion. I first decided to focus on ritual, because ritual is far more conservative than ideology and certainly more identifiable. Ritual can be observed, even by one who does not understand its symbolism and intent; whereas ideology is subject to responses from informants who may be seeking to mislead the questioner, may misunderstand the questions, may be uninterested or inarticulate, or may simply seek to amuse her- or himself at the expense of the questioner. I am aware of each of these circumstances having taken place in regard to Native Americans.

Furthermore, history can become blurred over time. For example, some of the Pueblo peoples assume tobacco came into their ceremonies after contact with the Spanish, when we know from the archeological evidence that the ancestors of the Pueblo people grew tobacco long before contact. More important, ethnologists can be blinded by their cultural blinkers; hence, their impression that women had little or no role in Native American religions.

To determine the history of the central ritual artifact in modern pan-Indian religion, the Sacred Pipe, I decided to survey the premodern pipes in ethnographic collections and those illustrated in early paintings and drawings. Both approaches have a number of inherent problems.

Foremost of these difficulties is the unreliability of most published material, in that no one had previously carried out a thorough survey of the whole of North America. Scholars had studied selected areas, such as Iroquoian culture and the Plains, but then had generalized their understanding, at times improperly. Others have written general works outside of their research competence. Hence, glaring errors have appeared in general works. For example, in a recent survey of Native American art, two pipes are illustrated and described as early nineteenth century, yet one is less than twenty years old and the other is late nineteenth century (Furst and Furst 1982).

MUSEUM RESEARCH

There are thousands of separate-stemmed pipes in the major ethnographic collections, but most have little, if any, data accompanying them, and where there is data, its reliability has to be ascertained. In my research, I sought four items of data. First, the earliest reliable date. Ideally, one would like to know when the pipe was manufactured and the dates of use. Usually all that is available is the date of museum acquisition, sometimes the date of ethnographic collection, and, rarely, a history of the pipe. Second, the culture of use. From a religious-studies perspective it is the culture that utilized the religious artifact that is of importance. This approach differs from that of the art historian, who is interested in the culture of manufacture. Many of the pipes were not made by the culture that used them at the time of collection. They may have been given by another group as a gift, traded, or even captured. This does not negate, indeed may even enhance, the Native regard for specific artifacts. Third, the location of collection. Ethnographic descriptions of Native people, especially those from before this century, tend to be vague. For example, the general appellation "Sioux" was given to an extensive set of cultures spread over a relatively large area. Sometimes this appellation is used for any artifact from the northern Plains in the United States. Fourth, the ritual use. This is the most difficult criterion of all and yet the most important. In some cases the determination is clear; for example, where the pipe is in sacred bundles or definitely associated with other ritual objects, or where there is precise ethnographic data about ritual use. In all other cases, the determination must be made by inference. One means is to note significant symbolic decoration; for example, a red ochre coating, the trachea or lifeline design, or suspended human scalps or an appropriate number of eagle feathers. These aspects of the artifact, combined with other data, may lead to varying probabilities of the ritual use of the artifact. Association with historic events, such as councils or adoption rituals, may also be of significance.

Of the thousands of pipes studied, exceedingly few met all four criteria. Examples were selected by their value to the study even with limited data. For example, when only one pipe was available for a particular culture, it was included in the study if at least one of the four items of data was known. However, since the focus was on ritual, ritual use was normally the determining factor for inclusion in the data base. Fewer than two percent of the pipes studied met this criterion. In total, including pipes known through illustrations, ritual use could be listed as definite or almost definite for 103 pipes and probable for another 54. It is to be understood that many more were undoubtedly used ritually, but there were no specific indicators. On the other hand, the majority of pipes in the collections, especially those with a large number of more recently acquired pipes, were manufactured at Pipestone, Minnesota for the tourist trade.

Care has to be exercised in doing this kind of museum research: labels and descriptions may be unreliable or have become confused. Items obtained from dealers normally cannot be used. For example, it is the standard procedure of at least some dealers to place bowls and stems together at random. At times, I found stem inserts were too large for the bowls. Bowls or stems may show no indication of having been smoked. (This does not apply to archeological examples, because ground scouring or the premodern museum tendency to clean objects may remove carbon traces and other signs of use.)

Data can also be lost over time. The objects transferred from the Army Medical Museum to the Smithsonian Institution when it began in 1867 had no virtually no data accompanying them. Lack of documentation limits the collection's usefulness. Heye, whose collection is now the Museum of the American Indian, was notorious for throwing away his field collector's notes, only the object being of interest to him. Hence, Heye's collection is the least reliably documented of those studied. The pipes collected by Lewis and Clark, who were meticulous in their descriptions, lost this information in their many transfers (thirteen pipes with six different cultures or subcultures). Although most, if not all, of the collection is now in the Peabody Museum, unfortunately the pipes cannot be matched to Lewis and Clark's identifications, and it is not even certain which stems belong to which bowls.

On the other hand, substantial parts of two of the museum collections, the Field Museum and the American Museum of Natural History, were collected by young ethnologists also studying the cultures. These collections were the most useful and reliable for this study.

Accessioning was sometimes rushed or careless and is subject to errors. A pipe in one major collection was first labeled as Seneca, which someone later changed to Huron. Fortunately, in the files was the original early-nineteenth-century letter that accompanied the pipe. In actuality, the pipe was from the Seminole. The person who originally accessioned the pipe over a century ago must have only looked at the first two or three letters.

All the artifacts studied were from major collections. Small local collections were sampled, but in all cases, there was insufficient data accompanying the artifacts for research purposes. Undoubtedly, in the many such collections, there will be some objects relevant to this study. However, given the nature of the conclusions, they could but enhance rather than contradict the findings. Finally, the emphasis on pipe bowls should be explained. As previously discussed, the assumption among early ethnologists that the stem is more important than the bowl is based on the "calumet dance," and it may well be true in one or two cultures, just as the opposite is in others. For the Sacred Pipe's primary religious function, which is to offer tobacco smoke to sacred entities, the bowl is indispensable. The kind of pipe bowl studied is usually made of stone or clay, far less perishable than the wooden stems. To bridge ethnographic and archeological collections one must focus on the bowls, since stems rarely survive burial or other exposure to the elements. Bowls are also subject to more stylistic variation, allowing stylistic analysis.

ILLUSTRATIONS

Illustrations can also be informative, but again must be used with caution. The most blatant example is that of the late-nineteenth century photographer in Washington, D.C., who photographed many of the Native dignitaries as they passed through the capital. To each he handed a pipe kept in the studio before taking the photograph. The most important paintings are by Bodmer and Catlin from the 1830s. Each was interested in material objects—Catlin was fascinated by pipes—and meticulous in portraying them accurately. Bodmer's illustrations are verified by the pipes Prince Maxmillian Zu Wied brought back from America, now in German museums. Catlin eventually did a portfolio on pipes alone. One can assume that the pipes Catlin's subjects chose to hold for their portraits were probably used by them in some aspect of ceremonial smoking; they differ considerably from those Catlin preferred to collect.

  Illustrations from early ethnological studies are also important, but again require a cautious approach. I will illustrate the point by one example from the works of Alanson Skinner, who was far more meticulous than most; for example, he himself pointed out that one of the pipes he collected for the Milwaukee Public Museum, labeled a "chief's" pipe, was never smoked (1926:238). On the other hand, he did determine the age of pipes by assuming whether they had been made by stone or metal tools. I was able to examine half of these pipes under magnification and was unable to detect a difference (except for one relatively modern at the time of collection). Well-made pipes are sanded, with sandpaper today and sandstone in the past, and do not often show tool marks. I do use drill hole styles as a criterion of age (conical boring with stone reamers as compared with straight holes from steel drill bits), and my conclusions are quite different from Skinner's dating.

The pipe in question (fig. 17) is labeled as an Iowa "Thunder-and-Eagle gens pipe" from Oklahoma. Skinner obtained the pipe from a collector in Missouri; the person the collector purchased it from many years previously was dead. The pipe was not wrapped as a sacred bundle and the stem had been repaired with wax. Skinner suggested the bowl did not belong with the relatively plain stem, but with the Buffalo gens pipe, whose bowl, described as similar to the one in question, was stolen "long ago." In summary, it is not even certain that the pipe is Iowa and its ritual association is certainly unclear. We are aware of these problems because Skinner informs us of them in his publication. Usually these doubts are not written down, and one has only the apparently certain statements of illustration labels and museum acquisition entries.

Due to the inherent potential for error in this type of research, conclusions should be based on a sufficient number of samples to obviate the effects of incorrect data, which is a statistical certainty. Even if as much as twenty-five percent of the data for the artifacts used in the distribution analysis were incorrect, which I think unlikely, the conclusions would still hold. The data base of 157 artifacts with certain or probable ritual association should be sufficient for the limited conclusions presented in this study. To keep the quality of the data as high as possible while the study progressed, entries with less information were replaced by entries with more complete or reliable information. Over time, the more than 600 original entries, already a small percentage of the pipes examined, were reduced to the 196 tabulated in Appendix II.

Data on Sacred Pipes

KEY

People, date, place. Ritual use. Bowl: shape, material, length, height, width (in centimeters); decor. Stem: shape, length, decor. Usage and other data. (Publication reference) Museum and reference number.

An asterisk denotes pipes illustrated in the text. *Place* refers to the place where the pipe was collected or depicted. The date is earliest for which there is data; otherwise, it is the date of acquisition (not to be understood as date of manufacture). *No data on ritual* use does not necessarily mean that ritual use was absent, only that it is not documented.

Selected entries focus on pipes with definite or probable ritual use; however, for cultures without such entries, or for entries relevant to preceding discussions, available data is entered.

MUSEUM ABBREVIATIONS

AMNH.	American Museum of Natural History (New York)
APM.	Alberta Provincial Museum (Edmonton)
BM.	British Museum (London)
BMA.	Brooklyn Museum of Art
CM.	Carnegie Museum (Pittsburgh)
EM.	Etnografiska Museet (Stockholm)
FM.	Field Museum of Natural History (Chicago)

GAM.   Glenbow-Alberta Museum (Calgary)
GI.   Gilcrease Institute (Tulsa)
ISHS.   Iowa State Historical Society (Des Moines)
LM.   Linden-Museum (Stuttgart)
MAI.   Museum of the American Indian, Heye Foundation (New York)
MPM.   Milwaukee Public Museum
NMI.   National Museum of Ireland (Dublin)
NMM.   National Museum of Man (Ottawa)
PM.   Peabody Museum of Archaeology and Ethnology (Cambridge)
ROM.   Royal Ontario Museum (Toronto)
SI.   Smithsonian Institution (Washington, D.C.)
UM.   Übersee Museum (Bremen)

SACRED PIPES

1. Abnaki, Maine, 1899. Ritual use probable. Bowl: keel, grey stone, 4.2, 5.2, 2.5; canoe inscribed on base, six beaver tails, six double ellipses, six dots inscribed on bowl, one hole and four point on keel. PM 55942.

2. Arapaho 1; 1875; Wyoming, Wind River Reservation. Ritual use highly probable. Bowl: one-piece, flat, yellow stone, 35.0; square top to round bowl. Arapaho tribal sacred pipe. (Carter 1938:94–95, fig. 10)

3. Arapaho 2; 1841; Nebraska, Oglala Station. No data on ritual use. Bowl: keel, steatite, 7.0, 10.7, 4.2. U.S. Army Medical Museum transfer. SI 8550.

*4. Arapaho 3; 1900; Wyoming, Wind River Reservation. No data on ritual use. Bowl: circular, grey stone, 4.4, - , 2.5, taper-bored. Stem: round, 48.5. FM 61457.

5. Assiniboine 1, 1832, Upper Missouri Basin. Ritual use highly probable. Bowl: slight-projection elbow, catlinite. Stem: round. Ill. in Catlin drawing *Pipe Dance of the Assiniboines*. (McKracken 1959:180)

6. Assiniboine 2, 1837, Upper Missouri Basin. Ritual use probable. Bowl: slight-projection elbow, catlinite. Stem: flat. Ill. in Catlin painting *Pigeon's Egg Head*. (Hassrick 1977:129)

7. Assiniboine 3; 1841; Dakota Territory, Fort Buford. Ritual use highly probable. Bowl: keel, black stone, 6.5, 14.8; six holes in keel, lead-repaired stem hole, brass-bound bowl top. Stem: round, 71.8, red "life" line, brass tacks (3 x 2, eight times), remnant of red cloth and sinew. Army Medical Museum transfer. SI 8495, T15929.

8. Assiniboine 4; 1974; Alberta, Alexis Reservation. Ritual use highly probable. Bowl: elbow, grey stone, 6.9, 4.7, 3.8, square stem, crude manufacture. Stem: round, 25.5, bark-covered. Made by Louis Aginaym, grand-

father of Peter Potts. Kept in family, in bag with sweetgrass braid. APM H74.117.1a-d.

9. Athabaskan (Beaver?); 1837; Northwest Territories, Fort Norman. Bowl: keel, grey-brown stone, 6.0; elaborate keel form. Stem: round, 12.0. (King 1977:96)

10. Bannock, Idaho (?). Bowl: slight-projection elbow, black stone, 7.8, 4.5, 2.5; thimble bowl, wide bore. Stem: flat, 36.8, notched decor. SI 200337.

11. Blackfoot 1; 1913; Alberta, Boket. Ritual use highly probable. Bowl: keel, black painted stone, 6.5, 13.0, 5.2; four points on keel. Necessary for Seed Dance. NMM V-B-279.

12. Blackfoot 2; 1966; Alberta, Blackfoot Reserve. Ritual use highly probable. Bowl: elbow, black stone, 6.5, 5.0, - ; heavily ochered. Stem: round, 29.0, heavily ochered. With plain, heavily ochered buckskin bag. Associated with Sun Dance. From Mary Water Chief, Sun Dance sponsor; museum kept pipe in locked sacred bundle cabinet. GAM AF713a-c.

13. Blackfoot 3, 1960, Alberta, Blackfoot Reserve. Ritual use highly probable. Bowl: elbow, catlinite, 8.5, 6.5, -; inlay on stem end, acute angle to elbow, hand-bored bowl. Stem: round, 23.0. In square rawhide bag with shell, three "buffalo" stones, fossilized prairie snail shell, and heavily ochered V-shaped stone. From holy man Jack Black Horse; kept in locked sacred bundle cabinet. GAM AF928bc.

14. Blackfoot 4; 1965; Alberta, Blackfoot Reserve. Ritual use highly probable. Bowl: straight, black stone, taper to rim and stem end, quilled rim. Has small quilled bag for bowl. Similar to bowl with Beaver Bundle pipe, which belonged to Arthur Little Light; obtained by museum on his death. APM H65.98.5a.

15. Blackfoot 5; 1965; Alberta, Blackfoot Reserve. Ritual use highly probable. Bowl: elbow, black stone. Stem: round, ochered. Belonged to Little Light (see No. 14); in cloth bag with sweetgrass and tamper. APM H65.225.6ab.

16. Blackfoot 6; 1965; Alberta, Blackfoot Reserve. Ritual use highly probable. Bowl: slight-projection elbow, grey stone, flat base, square projection, cylindrical bowl. Stem: round. Horn Society Sacred Bundle Pipe. APM H65.101.2ab.

17. Blackfoot 7; 1965; Alberta, Blackfoot Reserve. Ritual use highly probable. Bowl: T-shaped, catlinite, 12.3, 10.0, 3.1; grooves on all ends. Given to museum to be kept in safe place. Used in Big Smoke Ceremony. APM H65.227.1ab.

18. Blackfoot 8; 1965; Alberta, Blackfoot Reserve. Ritual use highly probable. Bowl: slight-projection elbow, dark grey stone, 8.9, 5.9, 2.6. Stem: round, 41.6. Horn Society Pipe from Mrs. Bear Hat. APM H65.99.2ab.

19. Blackfoot 9; 1960; Alberta, West Camp. Ritual use highly probable. Bowl: T-shaped, dark stone, 17.8, 9.4, 2.7; two rings on projection and bowl

end, three rings on stem end, "WC" carved on base, flat base. Stem: round, 39.9. In fetus skin bag. Part of Tobacco Society Bundle. ROM 960.270.96a-e.

20. Blackfoot 10, 1843, Rocky Mountains. Ritual use probable. Bowl: keel, steatite, 4.5, 10.3, 2.3. Stem: round, 85.4. With leather bag for bowl; said to have belonged to chief. EM 1854.2.20.

*21. Blood 1; 1903; Montana, Blood Reservation. Ritual use highly probable. Bowl: straight, catlinite, 8.7, -, 2.0; slight taper to bowl end. Stem: round, 35.5, wrapped with mink fur and four large blue glass beads, two large eagle and cardinal feathers pendant. Beaver pipe; collected by Wissler. AMNH 50/5413.

22. Blood 2; 1904; Montana, Blood Reservation. Ritual use highly probable. Bowl: keel, grey stone, seven points on keel, stained red. Stem: round, total length pipe 30.0, stained red. Sweetgrass braid looped and tied to stem. Used by women in Horn Society transfer ceremony. (Wissler 1916:415, fig. 22). AMNH 50/5410A.

23. Blood 3; 1897; Alberta, Blood Reserve. Ritual use probable. Bowl: keel, grey stone, 5.2, 9.4, 3.2; flange, four points on projection end. Stem: round, 57.0, two bands of brass wire. Belonged to Chief Red Crow. FM 51594.

*24. Blood 4; 1897; Alberta, Blood Reserve. Ritual use highly probable. Bowl: keel, steatite, 10.0, 14.0, 5.0; 2 inlaid dots stem end, four holes in keel, complex circle and dot (sun?) pattern, huge double tapered bowl. Stem: round, 71.5 FM 51632.

25. Blood 5; 1968; Alberta, Blood Reserve. Ritual use highly probable. Bowl: keel, black stone, 4.1, 4.2, 2.1; no keel, ochered. Stem: round, 21.3, ochered. Motoki (Women's) Society pipe. APM H68.182.2ab.

26. Blood 6; 1900; Alberta, Blood Reserve. Ritual use highly probable. Bowl: slight-projection elbow, catlinite, slight taper to bore and bowl. Stem: round, eight rows of tacks, blue and yellow beads, ribbons and horsehair. Secondary pipe of "Long Time Medicine Pipe Bundle," earliest known ceremonial bundle, still considered holy. APM H67.236.96.

27. Blood 7; 1965; Alberta, Blood Reserve. Ritual use highly probable. Bowl: keel, black stone, 2.0, 2.8, 1.4; five points on keel. Stem: round, 11.6. With small ochered and beaded bag; Horn Society Pipe from Laurie Plume. APM H65.212.3ab.

28. Cayuse; 1900; Oregon, Umatilla Reservation. No data on ritual use. Bowl: circular, light red stone, 5.6, 2.5. FM 61970.

29. Cherokee, 1725, South Carolina. No data on ritual use. Bowl: large-projection elbow, steatite, upturned projection, no flange. Collected by Sir Francis Nicholson, governor of South Carolina, 1721–25. (King 1977:26) BM S1.1214.

30. Cheyenne, Northern 1; 1911. Ritual use highly probable. Bowl: straight, catlinite. Stem: round. Pipe of Box Elder's Straight Pipe Bundle, still in use. (Powell 1969:II, 452; mentioned by Grinnell)

31. Cheyenne, Northern 2; 1832; Upper Missouri. Ritual use probable. Bowl: slight-projection elbow, catlinite. Stem: flat, quillwork, horsehair. Ill. by Catlin in drawing of pipe of Chief Nee-hee-o-woo-tis, who made and refused to sell the pipe. His wife decorated the stem. (Ewers 1979: pl. 4)

32. Cheyenne, Southern 1; 1903; Oklahoma, Eagle City. Ritual use highly probable. Bowl: straight, black stone. Stem: round. Photographed in use during sun dance. (Dorsey 1905:76)

33. Cheyenne, Southern 2; 1870; Oklahoma. Ritual use probable. Bowl: pointed-projection elbow, steatite, 17.5, 8.2, 4.0; lead and catlinite inlay, square stem, tapered projection, tapered bore. Collected by Harrington. Inscribed pipe of Wolf Chief, Medicine Man and Chief, 1870. MAI 2/2527.

*34. Cheyenne, Southern 3; 1904; Oklahoma. Ritual use highly probable. Bowl: straight, catlinite, 9.2, -, 2.4; carved ring at stem end. Stem: round, ochered. Collected by Mooney. Pipe from Red Cloud's Sun Dance bundle. FM 96821.

35. Choctaw; 1830; Alabama, Dancing Rabbit Creek. Ritual use highly probable. Bowl: effigy, stone, height 10.3; head facing away from stem. Archaic pipe from Mississipian period. Used at treaty of Dancing Rabbit Creek. GI 6125.1739.

36. Comanche. Ritual use probable. Bowl: slight-projection elbow, grey stone, 9.5, 6.0, 3.1; six-sided bowl, repaired with sinew. Stem: round, 21.1, ochered. MAI 2/1361.

37. Cree, Eastern 1; 1915; Quebec, Great Whale River. No data on ritual use. Bowl: keel, soapstone, height 8.6; incised circles. Stem: round, 14.6, hanging beadwork. (Brasser 1976, pl. 182) NMM III-D-28.

38. Cree, Eastern 2; 1904; James Bay. No data on ritual use. Bowl: slight-projection elbow, steatite, 13.0, 6.8, 3.5; four rings inlaid on stem. Stem: not original. AMNH 50/5283.

39. Cree, Eastern 3; 1910; Ontario. Ritual use probable. Bowl: pointed-projection elbow, steatite, 11.6, -, 2.5; inlaid, flange. Stem: round, puzzle type, quillwork, beads and horsehair, four eagle feathers pendant. ROM HD18 (913.15.18).

40. Cree, Eastern 4; 1913; Ontario, Moose Factory. No data on ritual use. Bowl: keel, steatite, 5.6, 7.4, 2.6; double-tapered bowl, axe keel with four half-circles and one hole, thong to stem. Stem: round, 31.0, fully beaded with pendant beads. NMM III-D-5.

41. Cree, Plains 1; Canada. Ritual use probable. Bowl: keel, grey stone, inlaid on each side of base with circle (sun?) over human figure, taper-bored stem, large bowl. MAI 7/2415.

42. Cree, Plains 2; 1900; Saskatchewan, Poorman Reserve. Ritual use highly probable. Bowl: slight-projection elbow, dark stone, 11.7, 7.5, 2.5; flat base. Stem: round, 32.5. Owned by family at least three generations. Collected by Brasser as ceremonial pipe. II-A-359ab.

43. Cree, Plains 3; 1910; Saskatchewan, Saddle Lake Reserve. Ritual use highly probable. Bowl: elbow/effigy, stone, face away from smoker, painted orange. "Used in Cree rituals . . . " Obtained by Albert Cardinal (ca. 1910) from Ojibwa near Rocky Mountain House, Alberta. (Pipe not Ojibwa, possibly Pueblo). GAM AP206ab.

44. Cree, Plains 4; 1870; Saskatchewan, Sakinay Reserve. Ritual use probable. Bowl: slight-projection elbow, black stone, two rings carved on both ends, flat base. Stem: flat. Owned by Cha-ca-chas, signer of Treaty No. 4. GAM AP186.

45. Cree, Plains 5; 1900; Saskatchewan, Poorman Reserve. Ritual use probable. Bowl: T-shaped, black stone, 15.3, 9.1, 2.9; flat base. Stem: round, 44.1. In family since nineteenth century, collected by Dusenberry in 1965. GAM AP111ab.

46. Cree, Plains 6; 1935; Saskatchewan, Star Blanket Reserve. Ritual use highly probable. Bowl: T-shaped, black stone, 8.5, 4.4, 2.1; octagonal bowl. Stem: round, 33.9, sweetgrass braid tied to stem with two thongs. In family several generations; used in ceremonies, especially for warding off thunderstorms. GAM AP871a-c.

47. Cree, Plains 7; 1880; Saskatchewan, Gordon Reserve. Ritual use probable. Bowl: elbow, catlinite, three rings carved on stem end. Stem: round to flat. Maker died in 1885. Pipe kept in family until 1950 by wife, daughter, and granddaughter of maker; used by women. GAM AP1052ab.

*48. Cree, Plains 8; 1979; Saskatchewan, Poorman Reserve. Ritual use highly probable. Bowl: T-shaped, catlinite, 15.2, 7.8, 2.5; two rings incised on all ends, folded sweetgrass braid and wool stroud (from blanket offered in rain dance) tied to bowl. Stem: round, 32.3, commercial cedar stem. With medicine pouch. APM H80.5.4ab.

49. Creek; ca. 1700; Alabama, Coosa-Tallagoosa. No data on ritual use. Bowl: long-projection elbow, catlinite, length 18.0; axe- shaped projection, flange. (Fundaburck 1957: pl. 106)

50. Crow 1, Montana. Ritual use highly probable. Bowl: one-piece effigy, red-black stone, 10.2, 3.0, 2.2; bison or bear, bowl is top of head, pipe smoked through tail. In ritual bundle. MAI 21/545.

51. Crow 2, 1900, Montana. Ritual use highly probable. Bowl: straight, incised. Stem: round; feathers and ribbons. In Pretty Coyote's medicine pipe. (Wildschut 1960: fig. 49, 50) MAI 11/6456.

*52. Crow 3, 1900, Montana. Ritual use highly probable. Bowl: straight, catlinite, 15.8, -, 2.5; lightning zigzag, Big Dipper, four rings on stem end. Stem: round, 33.6. Standing Bull's medicine pipe. (Wildschut 1969: fig. 47, 48) MAI 11/7698.

53. Crow 4, 1900, Montana. Ritual use highly probable. Bowl: straight. Stem: round. Accompanied effigy. (Wildschut 1969: fig. 16) MAI 11/6466.

*54. Crow 5, 1901, Montana. Ritual use highly probable. Bowl: straight, catlinite, 18.3, 2.2, 2.7; square shape, Big Dipper or Pleiades, crude horses' hooves, tapered bowl and stem bore. Stem: round, 43.1, design from burning. FM 69554.

55. Crow 6, Montana. Ritual use highly probable. Bowl: slight-projection elbow, steatite, 17.6, 9.0, 3.1; elaborate inlay, square stem. Stem: round, 42.0, trachea design similar to Skidi Pawnee design in ritual bundle (MAI 24/1120). MAI 24/2250.

56. Crow 7, Montana. No data on ritual use. Bowl: keel, grey stone, 3.6, 6.1, 1.9. MAI 18/9244.

57. Crow 8, Montana. Ritual use highly probable. Bowl: elbow, catlinite, 10.2, 9.0, 2.3; three rings on stem and bowl, slight obtuse angle, tall non-tapered bowl. Stem: flat, 48.3; human hair locks, ermine, six eagle feathers. MAI 23/278.

58. Crow 9, Montana. Ritual use highly probable. Bowl: slight- projection elbow, catlinite, 15.8, 8.7, 4.4; tapered bowl. Stem: round, 73.0, straight groove with red ochre (lifeline). MAI 0/7771.

59. Delaware, 1653, mid-Atlantic coast. Ritual use probable. Bowl: keel/proto? Stem: round, over one meter in length. Ill. in 1653 drawing by Peter Martensson Lindstrom in Riksarkivet, Stockholm. (King 1982:68, fig. 73)

60. Dogrib, 1868, Northwest Territories. No data on ritual use. Bowl: elbow, steatite, 9.5, 6.5, 2.6; four rings at top and two rings at stem end, stem end octagonal, taper-bored; trumpet-shaped bowl, fine-line incising of diamonds. SI 6200.

61. Flathead, Montana. No data on ritual use. Bowl: slight-projection elbow, light green stone; 9.2, 6.1, 2.5. MPM 30948.

62. Fox 1, 1920. Ritual use highly probable. Bowl: slight-projection elbow, catlinite, flange. Stem: round, feathers and hair. Part of Sacred Owl Bundle. (Michelson 1921: pl. 4)

63. Fox 2, Iowa. No data on ritual use. Bowl: slight-projection elbow, steatite, 14.0, 7.7, 3.5; inlaid bird on flange. Stem: flat, 47.0, rawhide and quillwork. Collected by Harrington. MAI 2/7874.

*64. Hidatsa 1, 1911, North Dakota. Ritual use highly probable. Bowl: one-piece flat, wood, disc rim. In Black Bear Bundle, used for eagle trapping. (Wilson 1928:225, fig. 18) AMNH 50.1/6018.

65. Hidatsa 2; 1890; North Dakota, Fort Berthold. No data on ritual use. Bowl: slight-projection elbow, grey stone, 19.1, 9.1, 3.7; square base. Stem: round. Collected from Sitting Bear by Grinnell. MAI 11/393.

66. Hidatsa 3; North Dakota, Fort Berthold. Ritual use highly probable. Bowl: slight-projection elbow, grey stone, 8.6, 6.2, 3.0; V on top with red color, flat base. Stem: round, 42.0. Museum reference number of Water Burst Clan, Buffalo Sacred Bundle, but no pipe listed on catalogue cards. MAI 7/8199.

67. Huron, 1825, near Quebec City. No data on ritual use. Bowl: pointed-projection elbow, catlinite, inlaid. Stem: round. Ill. in painting by Edward Chatfield, *Three Chiefs of the Huron Indians, Residing at la Jeune Lorette, near Quebec* in Public Archives of Canada.

68. Illinois, 1673, New France. Ritual use probable. Bowl: keel, developed style, one hole in keel, thong to stem. Stem: round, thin, quilled? (GI manuscript collection, Nicolas 1675, 5)

69. Iowa 1, 1832. Ritual use probable. Bowl: semi-disc, catlinite, pointed projection. Stem: flat. Ill. in Catlin painting *Man of Sense.* (Hassrick 1977:97)

70. Iowa 2, 1922, Oklahoma. Ritual use highly probable. Bowl: elbow/effigy, catlinite, lenght 12.0; animal-head bowl top facing smoker, flange may be broken off. Stem: round, 110.0, seven woodpecker scalps, etc. Pipe bundle of Pigeon gens. (Skinner 1926) MPM 30137.

71. Iowa 3, 1922, Oklahoma. Ritual use highly probable. Bowl: elbow/effigy, catlinite, length 13.0; animal-head bowl top facing smoker, high flange with three holes. Stem: flat, 100.0, quillwork, feathers. Pipe bundle of Tie (Buffalo) gens. (Skinner 1926) MPM 30356.

72. Iowa 4, 1922, Oklahoma. Ritual use highly probable. Bowl: slight-projection elbow, catlinite, 14.7, 7.8, - ; lizard on top of stem facing smoker, square rim around bowl top. Stem: round, fully quilled. Pipe of Wolf gens. (Skinner 1926) MPM 30532.

73. Iowa 5, 1922, Oklahoma. Ritual use highly probable. Bowl: elbow/effigy, catlinite, 15.8, 8.0, -; Janus-type head as bowl, animal flange facing smoker. Stem: round, feathers and ribbons. Pipe of Black Bear gens. (Skinner 1926) MPM 30531.

*74. Iowa 6, 1922, Oklahoma. Ritual use highly probable. Bowl: double-bowl elbow, catlinite, length 17.8, pointed projection, slight flange. Stem: round, ribbons. Possibly pipe of Thunder- Eagle gens. (Skinner 1926) MPM 31492.

*75. Iowa 7, 1922, Oklahoma. Ritual use highly probable. Bowl: slight-projection elbow, catlinite, 18.5, 9.0, - ; large flange, six double points and four heart cutouts, tapered bowl, nearly straight bore. Stem: round, many different feathers. Possibly pipe of Black Bear gens. (Skinner 1926) MPM 30143.

76. Iroquoian; ca. 1500; New York, Ontario County, Reed Fort Site. Ritual use highly probable. Bowl: disc, catlinite, length 16.8. Ceremonially "killed" in grave. (Hamilton 1967:25, fig. 15c)

77. Iroquoian, Neutral 1; Ontario, Wentworth County, Lake Medad. Ritual use highly probable. Bowl: disc, steatite, - , 10.0, 7.6; effigy otter or water spirit on rim with "lifeline" from mouth. MAI 5/7025.

78. Iroquoian, Neutral 2; Ontario, Wentworth County, Lake Medad. Bowl: keel, steatite, height 5.7; one hole. MAI 5/7025.

79. Iroquois, Cayuga; 1947; Ontario, Six Nations Reserve. Ritual use highly probable. Bowl: elbow, catlinite. Collected by Witthoft from Jerry Arrend, Cayuga. Part of a medicine bundle. (Witthoft 1953: pl. 2, no.5)

80. Kansas, 1832, Kansas. Ritual use probable. Bowl: double-bowl elbow, catlinite, slight projection. Stem: flat, quillwork, Ill. in Catlin drawing *Konza Warriors, Woman and Child.* (McKracken 1959:34)

81. Kaw, Oklahoma. No data on ritual use. Bowl: slight-projection elbow, steatite, 15.3, 8.3, 3.6; elaborate inlay. Stem: flat, 56.0, late, quillwork, ribbons, feathers, horsehair. Collected by Harrington. MAI 3/3566.

82. Kickapoo, 1910, Oklahoma. No data on ritual use. Bowl: elbow, white stone, 6.8, 5.9, 2.9. Stem: round, 24.1, square mouth end. Bought from Harrington. EM 1910.11.13.

83. Kiowa, Oklahoma. No data on ritual use. Bowl: slight-projection elbow, catlinite, 13.1, 9.4, 3.1; rings on bowl and stem. Stem: flat, 60.4, quillwork and faded ribbons. Collected by Harrington. MAI 10/3165.

84. Kutenai, 1970, British Columbia. No data on ritual use. Bowl: elbow, steatite, 8.0, 5.0, 2.2; wide rim around stem, thin bowl wall. PMA H70.185.2.

85. Mandan 1, 1830, North Dakota. Ritual use probable. Bowl: elbow, catlinite, length 12.0; sharp angle at bend. Stem: round, horsehair, six pendant feathers. (Coe 1976:500) Hermann Vonbank Collection.

86. Mandan 2, 1832, Upper Missouri. Ritual use probable. Bowl: slight-projection elbow, catlinite. Stem: round, eight eagle feathers pendant, blue beads. Ill. in Catlin painting *Pipes of Ha-na-tah Nu-maulik, Peace Chief.* (Ewers 1979:17)

87. Mandan 3, 1832, Upper Missouri. Ritual use probable. Bowl: slight-projection elbow, catlinite. Stem: round, seven eagle feathers pendant, white beads. Ill. in Catlin painting *Pipes of Ha-na-tah Nu-maulik, Peace Chief.* (Ewers 1979:17)

88. Mandan 4, 1832, Upper Missouri. Ritual use probable. Bowl: slight-projection elbow, catlinite. Stem: flat, three eagle feathers pendant, red feathers. Ill. in Catlin painting *Pipes of Ha-na-tah Nu-maulik, Peace Chief.* (Ewers 1979:17)

89. Mandan 5, 1832, Upper Missouri. Ritual use probable. Bowl: slight-projection elbow, catlinite. Stem: flat, quillwork, red feathers. Ill. in Catlin painting *Pipe of Mah-to-to-pah, War Chief.* Ewers 1979:18)

*90. Menomini 1; 1911; Wisconsin, near Green Bay. Ritual use highly prob-
able. Bowl: T-shaped, catlinite, 30.1, 12.0, 2.9; stem end 9 cm. square.
Stem: round, spiral mouth half, painted blue, green, red, yellow. Pipe
from war bundle. AMNH: 50.1/5853.

91. Menomini 2; 1912; Wisconsin, near Green Bay. Ritual use highly probable. Bowl: slight-projection elbow, catlinite, 15.6, 9.7, 3.0; two rings at
each end of bowl, slight double taper. Stem: flat, 65.1, stained red.
"Peace pipe of tribe." (Skinner 1913:23, fig. 1) AMNH 50.1/6622.

92. Menomini 3, Wisconsin, near Kenosha. Ritual use highly probable. Bowl:
slight-projection elbow, catlinite, 15.1, 8.8, 4.0; conical bowl. Stem: flat,
87.0, spiral twist. Handwritten on old paper pasted on stem, "given to
person on adoption as child." MAI 24/2236.

*93. Menomini 4; 1910; Wisconsin, Menomini Reservation. Ritual use highly
probable. Bowl: elbow, black stone, 5.5, 5.2, 3.1; rim around stem end
and bowl, large bore. Stem: flat, 38.2, elaborate cutouts, incised on one
side with turtle and "WAHKEY," on the other side with lightning. Note
by Barrett: "received as a result of a vision and was particularly used by
smoker . . . to appease the wrath of the thunder spirits." MPM 4447.

94. Menomini 5, 1911, Wisconsin. Ritual use highly probable. Bowl: pointed-
projection elbow, catlinite, 9.6, 6.3, 2.5. Stem: round, 27.0, with two
"joints." Collected by Skinner. Pipe of Thunder Drum outfit. AMNH
50.1/5907L.

*95. Menomini 6, 1911, Wisconsin. Ritual use highly probable. Bowl:
T-shaped, catlinite, 16.8, 9.5, 2.5; slight taper to bowl and bore. Collected by Skinner. Second Pipe of Thunder Drum outfit. AMNH
50.1/5907M.

96. Minataree 1; 1833; Upper Missouri, Fort Clark. Ritual use probable. Bowl:
pointed-projection elbow, catlinite, four inlaid bands on bowl, three on
stem, two hemispherical projections on bottom sides of bowl. Stem: flat
with horsehair and quills. Ill. in Bodmer painting of Pehiska-Ruhpa.
(Maximillian 1982:222)

97. Minataree 2, 1832, Upper Missouri. Ritual use probable. Bowl: slight-
projection elbow, catlinite. Stem: flat with horsehair and quills. Ill. in
Catlin drawing of Euh-tonk-pah-shee-pee-shah, Head Chief. (McKracken
1959:115)

98. Missouri 1, 1832. Ritual use probable. Bowl: pointed-projection elbow,
catlinite, bear (?) on flange facing away from smoker. Stem: flat, quillwork. Ill. in Catlin painting *He Who Likes the Osages.* (Hassrick 1977:
75)

99. Missouri 2, 1925, Oklahoma. Ritual use highly probable. Bowl:
T-shaped, catlinite, 15.0, 7.2, -; stippled design, straight bore. Stem:

flat, quillwork, hair, tacks. Female Buffalo gens pipe. (Skinner 1926) MPM 30147.

100. Montagnais; 1925; Quebec, Lake St. John. Ritual use probable. Bowl: keel, Montagnais-Nascapi type, slate, height 8.3; tassels from hole. Stem: round. MAI 2/8888.

101. Naskapi; 1925; Labrador, Moisie. Ritual use probable. Bowl: keel, Montagnais-Naskapi type, slate, height 7.6. Stem: round, loomed beadwork hanging to stem. Collected by Speck. MAI 3/2431.

102. Navajo, ca. 1875, New Mexico. Ritual use highly probable. Bowl: T-shaped, catlinite, 20.2, 7.7, 2.8; ten diagonal lines on sexagonal projection; inlaid inverted points on bowl top, band and four diamonds on stem end. Stem: round, 42.8; ten and fourteen brass tacks. Brought by Sioux to Navajo and Ute planning to join in an uprising, but they did not join it. When Sioux later came to urge others to join the Ghost Dance, the Navajo used the pipe in council. PM 62816.

103. Nez Perce; 1905; Washington, Colville. No data on ritual use. Bowl: T-shaped, catlinite. Stem: round. Seen in photograph of Yellow Bull, June, 1905. (Gidley 1979:75)

104. Ojibwa 1, Odawa, or Potowatami; 1800; Ontario, Amherstburg, Fort George. No data on ritual use. Bowl: elbow, catlinite, 11.0, 7.5, 2.3; octagonal bowl and stem, inlay on stem end and top. Collected by Jasper Grant. (Phillips 1984:74) NMI 1902–361.

105. Ojibwa 2, Odawa, or Potowatami; 1800; Ontario, Amherstburg, Fort George. No data on ritual use. Bowl: elbow, catlinite, 11.0, 6.3, 3.0; octagonal bowl and stem, elborate stem end. Collected by Jasper Grant. (Phillips 1984:74) NMI 1902–360.

106. Ojibwa 3, Odawa, or Potowatami; 1800; Ontario, Amherstburg, Fort George. No data on ritual use. Bowl: keel, black stone, 6.0, 10.0, 2.0, inlay on top and bottom, four appendages on keel. Collected by Jasper Grant. (Phillips 1984:74) NMI 1902–363.

*107. Ojibwa 4, 1813, Ontario, Niagara. No data on ritual use. Bowl: elbow, steatite, 12.0, 7.1, 3.6; extensive inlay, flange. Collected by Gen. Sir Gordon Drummond. NMM III-G-1098.

*108. Ojibwa 5, 1830. Ritual use probable. Bowl: elbow, grey stone, 10.0, 7.3, 3.5; four ridges on stem end, vestigial flange, octagonal stem, tapered bowl and bore. Stem: round, 89.6; six quilled eagle feathers pendant, quill-wrapped. In collection of Duke von Coburg-Gotha. NMM III-G-826ab.

109. Ojibwa 6, 1850. No data on ritual use. Bowl: keel, stone, inlay, four points on keel. Stem: round, thin, completely quill-wrapped, thong bowl to stem. (King 1982:71, fig. 76d)

110. Ojibwa 7, 1856. No data on ritual use. Bowl: pointed-projection elbow, steatite, flange with four cutouts, ridges on both ends, tapered base and bore, square base. NMM III-G-825.

111. Ojibwa 8, 1862, Minnesota. No data on ritual use. Bowl: T-shaped, catlinite, length 18.5; inlay, elaborate carving, slight tapered projection. One of earliest collected T- shapes. (Coe 1976:175)

112. Ojibwa 9; 1903; Minnesota, Leach Lake Reservation. Ritual use highly probable. Bowl: pointed-projection elbow, steatite, tapered barrel and bore. Stem: round, "lifeline" of triangles pointed away from smoker. FM 84400.

113. Ojibwa 10; 1903; Minnesota, Bois Fort. Ritual use probable. Bowl: pointed-projection elbow, steatite, extensive inlay of tree decor on stem end, flange with seven holes. Stem: flat to round, cut spiral, tacks. Bowl symbolism implies Midewiwin. AMNH 50/4696.

114. Ojibwa 11; 1919; Ontario, Lac Seul. Ritual use highly probable. Bowl: elbow, steatite, 8.0, 6.0, 3.1; diagonal grooves on both ends, square diamond incised on stem end. Stem: round, 9.2, bark-covered, probably not original stem. Used in Midewiwin rituals. NMM III-G-358b.

115. Ojibwa, Plains 1; 1875; Frank-Nut Lake Reservation. Ritual use probable. Bowl: T-shaped, catlinite, 15.3, 8.3, 2.3; four ridges on all ends. Stem: round, 45.5, one brass tack. Three generations in family of Old Yellow Bull, Salteaux Treaty signer. GAM HP2795ab.

116. Ojibwa, Plains 2; 1935; Saskatchewan, Fishing Lake Reserve. Ritual use probable. Bowl: elbow, catlinite, 6.2, 5.7, 2.3; taper-bored, repaired with solder. Stem: round, 20.0. Given to Albert Desjarlais by his father in 1935. PMA H72.19.6ab.

117. Omaha 1, 1832, Missouri Basin. Ritual use probable. Bowl: pointed-projection elbow, catlinite. Stem: round, red horsehair, feathers. Ill. in Catlin painting of Double Walker. (Hassrick 1977:77)

*118. Omaha 2, 1888, Nebraska. Ritual use highly probable. Bowl: slight-projection elbow, catlinite, 12.5, 7.2, 2.7; design (?) on stem with four lines, slight flange with thong to bowl, bowl blackened front and rear but not sides. Stem: round, 89.6. Used by Hangagens during hunting ritual; pipe named "Ni-ni-ba." PM 47838.

*119. Omaha 3, 1884, Nebraska. Ritual use highly probable. Bowl: elbow, catlinite, 10.3, 5.6, 3.3; high flange with hole, conical bowl and bore. Stem: flat, 111.5, slightly incised elliptical lines. In Sacred Tent of War Bundle. PM 37551 (same as Omaha 4)

*120. Omaha 4, 1884, Nebraska. Ritual use highly probable. Bowl: elbow, catlinite, 13.0, 5.5, 3.0; full length flange with six points and one hole, rim around bowl top, conical bowl and bore. Stem 1: round, 97.5; stem

2: flat 114.5, horsehair tied to middle. In Sacred Tent of War Bundle. PM 37551 (same as Omaha 3)

121. Oneota; ca. 1650; Missouri, Saline County, Utz Site. Ritual use highly probable. Bowl: T-proto, catlinite, tapered projections, flange, double-taper. (Wedel 1959: fig. 11c from middle grave skeleton, grave #8) ISHS 13Ae6–1032.

122. Osage 1. Ritual use highly probable. Bowl: disc, catlinite, -, 9.5, 3.6; four bone and three copper beads pendant. Stem: round, 58.5, thong to bowl, feather pendant remnant, hide wrap at mouth end. In ritual bundle. (West 1934: pl. 153) CM 70687.

*123. Osage 2; 1902; Oklahoma, Osage Reservation. Ritual use highly probable. Bowl: slight-projection elbow, catlinite, 9.5, 5.7, 2.9; two bands at each end, tapered bowl and bore. Stem: flat, 34.5, piece of scalp tied to stem, ochered. FM 71718.

124. Osage 3; 1901; Oklahoma, Osage Reservation. Ritual use highly probable. Bowl: slight-projection elbow, catlinite, inlay of triangles, tapered bowl and bore. Stem: round, scalp piece on thong, ochered. FM 59158.

*125. Osage 4, 1911, Oklahoma. Ritual use highly probable. Bowl: disc, catlinite 11.1, 3.1, 7.4; two triangles on projection, one hole, square base (a second identical pipe with stem is missing from museum). Stem: round, 47.7, zigzag line along length. Part of ritual bundle. BMA 06.64A.

126. Osage 5; 1916; Nebraska, Lincoln. Ritual use highly probable. Bowl: pointed-projection elbow, catlinite, 14.0, 7.9, 4.4; inlay on bowl and stem, two rings and six ribs to line stem top, conical bore and bowl. War bundle pipe collected by La Flesche from Mi-da'-in-ga of Tsi'-zhu wa-shta-ge gens. PM 86875.

127. Oto, 1832. Ritual use probable. Bowl: slight-projection elbow, catlinite. Stem: round, horsehair, red feathers. Ill. in Catlin painting of Loose Pipe-stem. (Hassrick 1977:103)

128. Odawa; 1880; Michigan, Cross Village. No data on ritual use. Bowl: keel, grey stone, three long rings around bowl. (Witthoft 1953: pl.2, no. 9)

129. Paiute; 1913; Nevada, Walker Lake. No data on ritual use. Bowl: straight, grey stone, -, 8.0, 2.6; beaded rim at stem end. Stem: round, 22.2, beaded band at pipe end, thong to bowl. PM 84672.

*130. Passamaquody 1, 1914, Maine. No data on ritual use. Bowl: keel, steatite, 1.9, 4.1, 1.5; four points on keel and one hole, double-tapered bowl. AMNH 50.1/7771.

*131. Passamaquody 2, 1916, Maine. Ritual use probable. Bowl: keel/effigy, steatite, 7.0, 11.7, 3.1; keel axe-shaped, bear facing away from smoker, oval bowl. Stem: round, 26.3, spiral groove. AMNH 50.1/9849.

*132. Pasamaquody 3, pre-1800, Maine. Ritual use highly probable. Bowl: keel/proto/effigy, steatite, 4.5, 15.1, 2.6. See Chap. 5 for description and analysis of decor. Dating by decor. AMNH 50.1/9850.

133. Paviotso; 1902; Nevada, Smith's Valley. Ritual use probable. Bowl: straight, grey stone, ring around stem end. Stem: round, wrapped with mink, ribbons. Overall length 35.5. FM 58460.

134. Pawnee 1, 1903, Skidi band. Ritual use highly probable. Bowl: T-shaped, catlinite. Stem: round, spiral black band (trachea). Pipe of Two Lance Society. (Murie 1914:566, fig. 5)

135. Pawnee 2, 1832, Missouri Basin. Ritual use probable. Bowl: slight-projection elbow, catlinite. Stem: flat, quills and horsehair. Ill. in Catlin painting *The Cheyenne*. (Hassrick 1977:111)

136. Pawnee 3, Oklahoma. Ritual use highly probable. Bowl: slight-projection elbow, catlinite, 10.5, 6.8, 3.1; four rings on bowl and stem, small flange. Stem: round, 48.1, trachea rings. From Eagle Chief's Bundle, obtained from his grandson. MAI 24/1120.

137. Pawnee 4; 1902; Oklahoma, Pawnee County. Ritual use highly probable. Bowl: pointed-projection elbow, catlinite, disc top bowl, tapered bowl, nine rings around stem end. Stem: round, thong to stem. From Scoo-rah Howe's bundle (two pipes). FM 71879.

138. Pawnee 5; 1902; Oklahoma, Pawnee County. Ritual use highly probable. Bowl: pointed-projection elbow, catlinite, flange with two heart cutouts, tapered bore. Stem: round. From Scoo-rah Howe's bundle (two pipes). FM 71880.

139. Pawnee 6; 1906; Oklahoma, Pawnee County. Ritual use highly probable. Bowl: slight-projection elbow, steatite, four rings on stem end, squarish stem, tapered bowl and bore. Stem: round, thong bowl to stem. From Bundle of Big Black Meteor (containing the famous star chart). FM 71898.

*140. Pawnee 7; 1902; Oklahoma, Pawnee County. Ritual use highly probable. Bowl: pointed-projection elbow, grey stone, 9.1, 6.5, 2.7; two grooves on stem end, curved projection. Stem: round, 65.7, burnished trachea stripes. From George Phillip's bundle. FM 71872.

*141. Pawnee 8; 1905; Oklahoma, Pawnee County. Ritual use highly probable. Bowl: T-shaped, catlinite, 20.8, 9.6, 3.2; double tapered bowl, tapered projection, straight drilled bowl. Stem: round, 59.1, thong from bowl to stem (second stem, 56.1, possibly used up). Bundle of Pahokatawa. FM 71897.

*142. Pawnee 9; 1915; Oklahoma, Pawnee Reservation. Ritual use highly probable. Bowl: elbow, steatite, 16.2, 8.9, 3.6; flange with eight points and five holes, square stem, tapered bowl and bore, incised ring around bowl top, thong, wrapped in buffalo wool. Pipe of Evening Star Bundle. AMNH 50.1/8421A.

143. Pawnee 10, 1915, Oklahoma, Pawnee Reservation. Ritual use highly probable. Bowl: T-shaped, catlinite, 16.0, 10.0, 3.0; straight bore and stem. Pipe of Kitkakuk bundle, only slightly used. AMNH 50.1/9706.

144. Pawnee 11, 1916, Oklahoma. Ritual use highly probable. Bowl: elbow, catlinite, flange with four notches and one hole, square rim, tapered bore and bowl. Stem: three round, one elaborate, two plain. Skull Bundle pipe. AMNH 50.2/185and179.

145. Penobscot, 1911, Maine, Old Town. No data on ritual use. Bowl: keel/effigy, steatite, animal facing away from smoker, thong hole, no keel but keel-type bowl. Stem: round, thong. AMNH 50/6052.

*146. Peigan, Northern; 1907; Alberta. Ritual use highly probable. Bowl: straight, catlinite, carved beaver on one side, incised lizard on the other, four rings on stem end, inlay repair and stem hole lining. Morris received the pipe from Chief Bull Plume: "Great Beaver Medicine Pipe (cost 10 horses)." (Morris 1985:35) ROM HK224.

147. Piegan, Southern 1; 1903; Montana. Ritual use highly probable. Bowl: keel, dark stone. Stem 1: round, fur and feathers; stem 2: plain. Medicine-pipe (Thunder) Bundle. Stem 1 used for Sun Dance; stem 2 for other rituals. (Wissler 1912:140, fig. 22) AMNH 40/5449a,d,o.

148. Piegan, Southern 2; 1900; Montana. Ritual use highly probable. Bowl: straight. Stem: round, decoration unclear. Ill. in drawing by bundle keeper. Pipe was part of Beaver Bundle owned by Tom Kiyo (1911) since the death of the previous carrier in 1901 at the reported age of 110. (Wissler 1912:170–71, fig. 25)

149. Piegan, Southern 3; 1908; Montana. Ritual use highly probable. Bowl: straight. Stem: round, decoration unclear. Ill. in drawing by bundle keeper. One of two pipes (the other is a keel pipe) in one of oldest Beaver Bundles. (Wissler 1912:170–71)

150. Piegan, Southern 4; Montana. Ritual use highly probable. Bowl: straight, four rings, thinner at stem end. Cather's Society Bundle. (Ewers 1963: 208)

151. Piegan, Southern 5. Ritual use highly probable. Bowl: slight-projection elbow, red stone, 15.4, 9.5, 2.6; catlinite and lead inlay of four-pointed star on stem end, cross of circles on bottom, birds ascending, moon; large crude bore. Stem: diamond-shaped, with incised arrow and four points. Cather's Society Bundle; one of two pipes, the second straight, but not seen by the author. May be No. 150. MAI 12/512.

152. Piegan, Southern 6; 1896; Montana. Ritual use highly probable. Bowl: keel. Pipe of Chief Three Suns. (Ewers 1963: pl. 21B)

153. Piegan, Southern 7; 1833; Upper Missouri. Ritual use probable. Bowl: keel, inlaid with four points on keel. Ill. in Bodmer painting of Piegan warrior. (Davis and Ronnefeldt 1982:137)

154. Peigan, Southern 8; 1965; Montana. Ritual use highly probable. Bowl: keel, grey stone. Stem: round. Motoki (Women's) Society Bundle. APM H65.74.1d-e.

155. Ponca, Oklahoma. No data on ritual use. Bowl: slight-projection elbow, catlinite, 14.5, 8.1, 2.8; two ridges on stem end, tapered bore and projection. Stem: flat, quillwork, ribbons, horsehair. MAI 23/9323.

156. Potowatami, 1925, Wisconsin. No data on ritual use. Bowl: elbow, grey stone, flange, three ribs on stem end, tapered bowl and bore. Stem: flat, puzzle, ribbons, red horsehair. FM 155722.

157. Salish (Thompson?); 1915; British Columbia, Thompson River. Ritual use probable. Bowl: elbow, grey stone, 11.9, 7.5, 3.2; inlaid with three rings around stem end, small projection at bottom of bowl with one hole; two snake rattles and one eagle down feather pendant, twelve lines of red ochre at stem end. Stem: round, 37.2, carving on bark. Possibly only bottom one-third of bowl heavily smoked. PM 86397.

158. Sarcee 1; 1900; Alberta, Sarcee Reserve. Ritual use probable. Bowl: T-shaped, catlinite, 10.1, 6.2, 2.2; four diagonal grooves on projection, rim around top of bowl, flat base, hand-bored. Collected by Sapir: "Crow Collar captured it from a Cree Indian in war." NMM V-D-334.

159. Sarcee 2; 1900; Alberta, Sarcee Reserve. Ritual use highly probable. Bowl: T-shaped, catlinite, 18.0, 8.1, 2.5; four ridges and octagonal projection, hand-enlarged bore. Stem: round, 44.7. Collected by Sapir in 1922. Used as a "peacepipe" by head chief, Bull Head (also called Little Chief), bought from his stepson. NMM V-D-159a-b.

*160. Sauk 1, 1830. Ritual use probable. Bowl: pointed- projection elbow, catlinite, 13.0, 6.4, -; flat base, hexagonal point, tapered bowl and bore. Used by Black Hawk. MPM 2761.

161. Sauk 2, 1833. Ritual use probable. Bowl: pointed-projection elbow, catlinite. Black Hawk's pipe given to President Jackson. (Ewers 1981:64, fig. 3) Speed Museum (Louisville).

162. Sauk 3, ca. 1830, Missouri River Valley. Ritual use probable. Bowl: slight-projection elbow, steatite, 12.4, 7.0, 3.1; inlay on bowl top, flange with one large hole, flat bottom, conical bowl. War Department transfer. Pipe from time of Black Hawk War? SI 2349.

163. Sauk 4, ca. 1830, Missouri River Valley. Ritual use probable. Bowl: slight-projection elbow, steatite, 12.1, 8.2, 3.5; flange with eight holes, flat bottom, conical bowl. War Department transfer. Pipe from time of Black Hawk War? SI 2422.

164. Seminole; 1839; Florida, Coloosahatche River. Ritual use probable. Bowl: slight-projection elbow/effigy, grey stone, 14.9, 6.8, 3.6; bear head projection facing away from smoker, two rings around top and one around stem, eight triangles on base painted red, blue and yellow; flange with

holes part broken. Accessioned as Seneca, original letter on file. Pipe found with returned possessions of trader killed on expedition to Seminole. PM 64511.

165. Shawnee 1, ca. 1800, Indiana. Ritual use probable. Bowl: slight-projection elbow, catlinite, 5.6, 3.9, 2.1; tapered bore. Owned by Tecumsah, obtained by Menomini chief who gave it to relative of a Mr. Gauthier, interpreter at Kenosha, Wisconsin, who gave it to Hoffman. (Hoffman 1896:248, fig. 32) SI 154377.

166. Shawnee 2; 1825; Illinois, Shawneetown. No data on ritual use. Bowl: long-projection elbow, catlinite, flange, tapered bowl. (Witthoft 1953: pl. 2, no. 7)

167. Shoshone; 1805; Idaho, Lemhi River. Ritual use highly probable. Bowl: straight, green stone, length 4.0, oval. Stem: wood, round, thin, 12.5. Ritually smoked with Lewis and Clark; crude drawing in Lewis and Clark's notebooks. (Thwaites 1956:II, 341–42)

*168. Sioux 1, Mdewakanton; 1851; Little Crow Village. Ritual use probable. Bowl: slight-projection elbow, catlinite, 15.7, 10.5, 4.5; extensive inlay, flat base, straight drilled bore and stem, slight conical bowl. Stem: flat, 93.4; middle part of flat stem carved into three round quill-wrapped tubes. Bowl and stem inscribed in German: "Belonged to Ce-tan-wa-hu-ava-muni [The One Who Always Hunts the Hawk] Sioux Chief, collected 19 May 1851." UM C8225.

169. Sioux 2, Mdewakanton; 1862; acquired in South Dakota, Pine Ridge Reservation. Ritual use probable. Bowl: pointed-projection elbow, steatite, 17.7, 9.8, 4.2; elaborate lead and catlinite inlay, flat bottom. Original paper label in bowl; owned by Little Crow Chief at rising in Minnesota, 1862. SI 378166.

170. Sioux 3, Santee; 1835. Ritual use probable. Bowl: slight- projection elbow, catlinite, inlay. Stem: flat, quillwork. Ill. in Catlin painting of Big Eagle. (Hassrick 1977:151)

171. Sioux 4, Teton; 1835. Ritual use highly probable. Bowl: elbow. Stem: round. Ill. in Catlin painting *Scalp Dance*. (Hassrick 1977:127)

172. Sioux 5, Teton; 1903; South Dakota, Pine Ridge Reservation. Ritual use probable. Bowl: straight, catlinite, circular ridges along entire length. Stem: round, twelve rings. Collected by Wissler. AMNH 50/4396.

173. Sioux 6, Teton; 1940; Cheyenne River Reservation. Ritual use highly probable. Bowl: long-projection elbow, catlinite, triangular flange with two holes, vertical triangular extension on projection, bowl slightly double tapered. Stem: round, birds, scalps, eagle feathers. White Buffalo Calf Pipe Bundle (denied by Lame Deer). (Thomas 1941: pl. 2)

174. Sioux 7, Teton; 1830; south of the Teton River. Ritual use highly probable. Bowl: elbow, catlinite, unclear decor. Stem: round, feathers and hair. Identified as a ritual pipe. (Catlin 1844:II, fig. 98a)

175. Sioux 8, Wahpekute; 1831; Minnesota, St. Peters. Ritual use probable. Bowl: pointed-projection elbow, catlinite, 9.0, 5.4, 3.0; slight flange, conical bowl and tapered bore. Stem: flat, green paint, part wrapped with gilt European cloth, edged with blue and white beads, red ribbons, *sweetgrass* tied to mouth end. Stem inscribed: "Wah ma de Sappah Chief 2nd of the Wahpacota June 20 1831." PM 53113.

176. Sioux 9, Wahpeton. Ritual use highly probable. Bowl: pointed-projection elbow, steatite, lead and catlinite inlay of horse on flange, squared stem, conical bowl, tapered bore. Listed as property of Wahpeton medicine man. SI 73072.

177. Sioux 10 (Yankton?), 1860. No data on ritual use. Bowl: T-shaped, catlinite, elaborate inlay, stippled with "1860" and buffalo design. Stem: flat, quilled, feathers. Assumed tourist pipe. (King 1977: 54) BM 1942.Am.7.1.

178. Sioux 11, 1835, Dakotas. Ritual use highly probable. Bowl: slight-projection elbow, catlinite. Stem: round, seven eagle feathers. Ill. in Catlin drawing, described as ritual pipe. (Ewers 1979: pl. 6)

179. Sioux 12, 1832, St. Pierre. Ritual use probable. Bowl: slight-projection elbow, catlinite. Stem: round, horsehair and feathers. Ill. in Catlin drawing *Shon-ka, Chief of the Ca-za-zhee-ta [Bad Arrow Points Band]*. (McKracken 1959:57)

180. Sioux 13 (possibly Gros Ventre), 1908, Montana. Ritual use probable. Bowl: slight-projection elbow, steatite, 10.0, 7.6, 2.5; tapered bore. Stem: flat, 52.7, red "lifeline", eight rows of red holes in stem end. Collected by Wissler; (paper in bowl "Gros Ventre" ?). AMNH 50/4869.

181. Sioux 14, before 1841, Upper Missouri. Ritual use probable. Bowl: effigy, catlinite, 9.3, 6.1, 2.9; horse head facing away from smoker, top is head of bowl, stem is inserted in neck; cone bored. War Department transfer. SI 6019.

*182. Sioux 15. No data on ritual use. Bowl: long-projection elbow, catlinite, 20.4, 6.2, 2.2. SI 359703.

183. Slave; Northwest Territories, McKenzie River. No data on ritual use. Bowl: keel, dark brown, 4.2, 5.4, 2.2; keel with four projections and one hole, tapered bore, brass band reinforcing bowl. SI T-17206.

184. Susquehannock 1; ca. 1650; Pennsylvania, Strickler site. Bowl: disc, steatite, 4.6, 6.6; round base. (Kent 1984:148, fig. 26)

185. Susquehannock 2; ca. 1700; Pennsylvania, Conestoga Town site. Bowl: long-projection elbow, catlinite, flange with four points and one hole. Another long-projection elbow pipe came from this site. (Kent 1984:153, fig. 30)

186. Susquehannock 3; ca. 1730; Pennsylvania, Lancaster County, Bainbridge, Hixon site. Bowl: keel, grey stone, double-tapered bowl, four holes in keel. From Conoy Town 1718–42. (Witthoft 1953: pl. 2, no. 19)

187. Tunica 1; 1731; Lower Mississippi. Ritual use highly probable. Bowl: long-projection elbow, catlinite, 13.0, 4.5, -; notched flange with two holes, frontal prow. Found in burial. (Brain 1979:248)

188. Tunica 2, 1731, Lower Mississippi. Ritual use highly probable. Bowl: elbow, catlinite, 5.0, 4.8, -; flange with hole, square stem. Found in burial; second elbow pipe also found. (Brain 1979:248)

189. Umatilla, 1913, Oregon. Ritual use probable. Bowl: elbow, black stone, 10.5, 5.5, 2.1; inlay on stem end forming four stone squares, slight projection at bottom. PM 8533.

*190. Unknown 1, ca. 1775. Ritual use highly probable. Bowl: elbow, catlinite, 3.2, 4.2, 1.9; ridge around top of bowl, slight knob at angle of bowl to base; incised effigies of elk or deer on bowl facing away from smoker, snake on one side of bowl, bird on the other; all with zigzag lines from mouth with split ends. Stem: round, 21.2, stained red, pipe end bound with sinew and piece of leather with three pendant beaded thongs ending with tin cones and red horsehair tied to pipe end with cord. Collected by Sir John Caldwell, who served in North America from 1774–80 and counciled with many Native cultures. NMM V-E-300ab.

191. Unknown 2, 1590, Florida. No data on ritual use. Bowl: pointed-projection elbow. Stem: round. Ill. by Debry in Brevis *Narrative*, published in Frankfort. (McGuire 1899:415, fig. 45)

192. Ute, 1875, Utah. No data on ritual use. Bowl: pointed- projection elbow, black stone, 6.7, 4.6, 2.4. Collected by Powell. SI 16785.

193. Winnebago 1; 1827; Butte de Morts. Ritual use probable. Bowl: slight-projection elbow, rings around bowl and stem. Stem: round, with six feathers. (Horan 1972:280–81)

194. Winnebago 2, 1835, Wisconsin, Green Bay. Ritual use probable. Bowl: keel. Stem: thin spiral. Ill. in Catlin painting *Man Who Puts All Out of Doors*. (Hassrick 1977:60)

195. Winnebago 3, 1854. Ritual use highly probable. Bowl: pointed-projection elbow. Stem: round, feathers and hair. Ill. in engraving by Alfred Jones (after Seth Eastman) *Medicine Dance of the Winnebago*. (McDermott 1961)

*196. Winnebago 4; 1908; Wisconsin, Black River Falls. Ritual use highly probable. Bowl: effigy, baby walrus tusk ivory, 10.7, 2.5, 1.9; four tiny inlaid dots, horse facing away from smoker, engraved and black-filled four-direction cross on top of stem end, groove along each side, ridged underside. Stem: thin round ivory, 10.2; four incised and filled lines.

Accepted as authentic by Dorsey. Part of a medicine bundle including rattles and eagle bone whistle. FM 14901.

REFERENCES

ADAIR, JAMES

    1775   *History of the American Indians.* London.

ADVASIO, J.M., AND R.C. CARLISLE

    1984   "An Indian Hunter's Camp for 20,000 Years." *Scientific American* 250(May): 130-37.

ALTER, J. CECIL

    1962   *James Bridger.* Norman: University of Oklahoma Press.

BAILEY, ALFRED GOLDSWORTHY

    1969   *The Conflict of European and Eastern Algonkian Cultures, 1504-1700.* Toronto: University of Toronto Press, 2nd ed.

BANCROFT-HUNT, NORMAN

    1981   *The Indians of the Great Plains.* London: Orbis.

BARRETT, S. A.

    n.d.   *Material Culture of the Menomine Indians.* Ms. the Milwaukee Public Museum.

BARTRAM, WILLIAM

    1853   "Observations on the Creek and Cherokee Indians." *Transactions of the American Ethnological Society* 3(1): 1-81.

BENNDORF, HELGA, AND SPEYER, ARTHUR

    1968   *Indianer Nordamerikas, 1760-1860.* Offenback A.M.: Deutschen Ledermuseum.

BENTON-BANAI, EDWARD

    1979   *The Mishomis Book.* St. Paul: Indian Country Press.

BERKHOFER, ROBERT F., JR.

    1978   *The White Man's Indian.* New York: Random House.

BERTHRONG, DONALD J.

1963 *The Southern Cheyennes*. Norman: University of Oklahoma Press.

BIRKET-SMITH, KAJ

1929 "Drinking Tube and Tobacco Pipe in North America." *Ethnotologische Studien* 1: 29-39.

BLACK ELK

1953 *The Sacred Pipe*. Edited by Joseph Epes

BROWN. NORMAN:

University of Oklahoma Press.

BLAKESLEE, DONALD J.

1981 "The Origin and Spread of the Calumet Ceremony." *American Antiquity* 46: 759-768.

BOUCHER, PIERRE

1664 *Histoire véritable et naturelle des moeurs et productions du pays de la Nouvelle France, vulgairement dite le Canada*. Paris: F. Lambert.

BOWDEN, HENRY WARNER

1981 *American Indians and Christian Missions, Studies in Cultural Conflict*. Chicago: University of Chicago Press.

BOWERS, ALFRED W.

1965 *Hidatsa Social and Ceremonial Organization. Bureau of American Ethnology, Bull.* 194.

BRAGGE, WILLIAM

1880 *Bibliotheca Nicotiana*. Birmingham: privately printed.

BRAIN, JEFFREY P.

1979 *Tunica Treasure. Papers of the Peabody Museum of Archaeology and Ethnology* 71.

BRASSER, TED J.

1976 *"Bo'jou, Neejee!": Profiles of Canadian Indian Art*. Ottawa: National Museum of Man.

1980 "Self-directed Pipe Effigies." *Man in the Northeast* 19: 95-104.

1987 "By the Power of Their Dreams, Artistic Traditions of the Northern Plains." *The Spirit Sings*. Calgary: Glenbow-Alberta Institute.

BRESSANI, F. J. (ATTRIBUTION)

1657 *Novae Francise Accurata Delineation*. (National Archives of Canada)

BROSE, DAVID S.

1985 "The Woodland Period." In *Ancient Art of the American Woodland Indians*, edited by Brose, Brown, and Penny. New York: Harry N. Abrams.

BROSE, BROWN, AND PENNY, EDS.

1985 *Ancient Art of the American Woodland Indians*. New York: Harry N. Abrams.

BURNETT, E. K.

1944   *Inlaid Stone and Bone Artifacts from Southern California. Contribu-tions to the Museum of the American Indian* 13.

BURPEE, L. J.

1910   *Journal of Larocque, from the Assiniboine to the Yellowstone, 1805. Publications of the Canadian Archives* No. 3. Ottawa.

BUSHNELL, DAVID I., JR.

1906   "The Sloan Collection in the British Museum." *American Anthropolo-gist* 8: 671-687.

CARTER, JOHN G.

1938   "The Northern Arapaho Flat Pipe and the Ceremony of the Covering the Pipe." *Anthropological Papers, No. 2. Bureau of American Ethnology, Bull.* 119: 69-102.

CARVER, JONATHAN

1778   *Travels Through the Interior Parts of North America in the Years 1766, 1767, and 1768.* London.

CATLIN, GEORGE

1844   *Letters and Notes on the Manners, Customs and Conditions of the North American Indians.* London.

CHAMPLAIN, SAMUEL DE

1922–   *The Works of Samuel de Champlain.* Edited by H. P. Biggar. Toronto:
1936   Champlain Society Publications.

CHARLEVOIX, PETER FRANCIS XAVIER DE

1761   *Journal of a Voyage to North America.* London.

COE, RALPH T.

1976   *Sacred Circles: Two Thousand Years of North American Indian Art.* London: Arts Council of Great Britain.

COOPER, JOHN M.

1957   *The Gros Ventres of Montana.* Edited by Regina Flannery. Washington D.C.: The Catholic University of America Press.

CORBETT, WILLIAM P.

1976   "A History of the Red Pipestone Quarry and Pipestone National Monument." M. A. diss., University of South Dakota.

CROSBY, ALFRED W., JR.

1972   *The Columbian Exchange, Biological and Cultural Consequences of 1492.* Conn.: Greenwood Press.

CULIN, STEWART

1911   "Brooklyn Institute Museum Report on a Collecting Trip Among the Indians of Oklahoma, New Mexico, California and Vancouver, May 3-July 28, 1911." Ms. Brooklyn Museum.

DAVIS, THOMAS, AND RONNEFELDT, KARIN

1982   *People of the First Man.* New York: Promontory Press.

DELORIA, VINE, JR.

1969 *Custer Died for Your Sins, An Indian Manifesto.* New York: MacMillan.

DENSMORE, FRANCES

1929 *Chippewa Customs. Bureau of American Ethnology, Bull.* 86.

DOCKSTADER, FREDERICK J.

1973 Indian Art of the Americas. New York: Museum of the American Indian.

DORSEY, GEORGE A.

1904 "Traditions of the Skidi Pawnee." *Memoirs of American Folklore Society* 8: 88-94.

1905 *The Cheyenne II: The Sun Dance. Field Columbian Museum, Anthropological Papers* 9(2).

DRINNON, RICHARD

1980 *Facing West, The Metaphysics of Indian-hating and Empire-building.* New York: New American Library.

DU PRATZ, LE PAGE

1758 *Histoire de la Louisiane.* Paris.

DUSENBERRY, VERNE

1962 *The Montana Cree: A Study in Religious Persistence.* Stockholm: Almqvist & Wiksell.

EWERS, JOHN C.

1963 *Blackfoot Indian Pipes and Pipemaking. Bureau of American Ethnology, Bull.* 186.

1965 *Artists of the Old West.* Garden City, N.Y.: Doubleday & Co.

1978 "Three Effigy Pipes by an Eastern Dakota Master Carver." *American Indian Art* 3(Autumn): 51-55.

1979 *Indian Art in Pipestone, George Catlin's Portfolio in the British Museum.* Washington, D.C.: Smithsonian Institution.

1981 "Pipes for the Presidents," *American Indian Art* 4 (Summer): 51-55.

1986 *Plains Indian Sculpture.* Washington, D.C.: Smithsonian Institution.

EWING, DOUGLAS C.

1982 *Pleasing the Spirits, A Catalogue of a Collection of American Indian Art.* New York: Ghylen Press.

FEDER, NORMAN

1964 *Art of the Eastern Plains Indians, the Nathan Sturges Jarvis Collection.* New York: Brooklyn Museum of Art.

FENTON, WILLIAM N.

1953 *The Iroquois Eagle Dance, An Offshoot of the Calumet Dance. Bureau of American Ethnology, Bull.* 156.

FEWKES, J. W.

1892 *Catalogue of the Hemenway Collection in the Historico American Exposition of Madrid. Report of the Columbian Historical Exposition.* Madrid.

FIEDEL, STUART J.

1987   *Prehistory of the Americas.* Cambridge: Cambridge University Press.

FLETCHER, ALICE C.

1904   "The Hako: A Pawnee Ceremonial." *22nd Annual Report, Bureau of American Ethnology, 1900-01.*

FLETCHER, ALICE C., AND LA FLESCHE, FRANCIS

1911   *The Omaha Tribe. 27th Annual Report, Bureau of American Ethnology, 1905-06.*

FREESOUL, JOHN REDTAIL, AND FREESOUL, RIVERWOMAN

1984   *Breath-Made-Visible: The Pipe as Spirit, Object & Art.* Sante Fe: Freesoul Art Studio.

FRISON, G. C.

1978   *Prehistoric Hunters of the High Plains.* New York: Academic Press.

FUNDABURK, EMMA LILA, AND FOREMAN, MARY DOUGLAS FUNDABURK

1957   *Sun Circles and Human Hands: The Southeastern Indians' Art and Industry.* Luverne, Alabama: Emma Lila Fundaburk.

FURST, PETER T.

1976   *Hallucinogens and Shamanism.* San Francisco: Chandler & Sharp.

FURST, PETER T., AND FURST, JILL L.

1982   *North American Indian Art.* New York: Rizzoli.

GAINES, GEORGE S.

1928   *Dancing Rabbit Creek Treaty.* Birmingham, Alabama: State Department of Archives and History, Historical and Patriotic Series No. 10.

GARTER SNAKE

1980   *The Seven Visions of of Bull Lodge.* Edited by George Horse Capture. Ann Arbor: Bear Claw Press.

GIDLEY, M.

1979   *With One Sky Above Us: Life on an Indian Reservation at the Turn of the Century.* New York: Putnam.

GILL, SAM D.

1982   *Native American Religions, An Introduction.* Belmont, Calif.: Wadsworth Publishing Co.

1987   *Mother Earth.* Chicago: University of Chicago Press.

GRANT, JOHN WEBSTER

1984   *Moon of Wintertime, Missionaries and the Indians an Encounter since 1534.* Toronto: University of Toronto Press.

GRINNELL, GEORGE BIRD

1889   *Pawnee Hero Stories and Folktales.* New York: Forest & Stream Publishing Co.

1908   *Blackfoot Lodge Tales.* New York: Charles Scribner & Sons.

HABERMAN, THOMAS W.

1984   "Evidence for Aboriginal Tobaccos in Eastern North America." *American Antiquity* 49: 269-287.

HALL, ROBERT L.

1977   "An Anthropocentric Perspective for Eastern United States Prehistory." *American Antiquity* 42: 499-518.

1983   "The Evolution of the Calumet Pipe." Edited by Guy E. Gibbon. *Prairie Archaeology: Papers in Honor of David A. Baerris. University of Minnesota Publications in Anthropology* 3.

HALLOWELL, A. IRVING

1960   "Ojibwa Ontology, Behavior, and World View." In *Culture in History*, edited by Stanley Diamond. New York: Columbia University Press.

HAMILTON, HENRY W.

1967   *Tobacco Pipes of the Missouri Indians. Missouri Archaeological Society Memoirs* 5.

HARNER, MICHAEL J.

1973   "The Sound of Rushing Water." In *Hallucinogens and Shamanism*, edited by Michael J. Harner. London: Oxford University Press.

HARRINGTON, JOHN P.

1932   *Tobacco Among the Karuk Indians of California. Bureau of American Ethnology, Bull.* 94.

HARRINGTON, M. R.

1922   *Cherokee and Earlier Remains on Upper Tennessee River. Indian Notes and Monographs.* New York: Museum of the American Indian.

HASSRICK, ROYAL B.

1977   *The George Catlin Book of American Indians.* New York: Watson-Guptill.

HENNEPIN, FATHER LOUIS

1698   *A New Discovery of a Vast Country in America.* Edited by R.G. Thwaites. Chicago: A. C. McClury, 1903.

HENRY, ALEXANDER

1809   *Travels and Adventures in Canadian and Indian Territories.* New York.

HOFFMAN, WALTER JAMES

1891   "The Mide'wiwin or 'Grand Medicine' Society of the Ojibwa." *7th Annual Report, Bureau of Ethnology, 1885-86*: 143-300.

1896   "The Menomini Indians." *14th Annual Report, Bureau of Ethnology, 1892-93:* 11-328.

HOLLER, CLYDE

1984   "Lakota Religion and Tragedy: The Theology of *Black Elk Speaks." Journal of the American Academy of Religion* 52: 19-45.

1984a   "Black Elk's Relationship to Christianity." *American Indian Quarterly* 7(4).

HOLMES, WILLIAM H.

1919   *Handbook of Aboriginal Antiquities, Part I. Bureau of American Ethnology, Bull.* 60.

HORAN, JAMES D.

1972   *The McKenney-Hall Portrait Gallery of American Indians.* New York: Crown.

HUDSON, CHARLES

1976   *The Southeastern Indians.* Knoxville: University of Tennessee Press.

HULTKRANTZ, ÅKE

1953   *Conceptions of the Soul Among North American Indians, A Study in Religious Ethnology.* Stockholm: Statens Etnografiska Museet.

1957   *The North American Orpheus Tradition, A Contribution to Comparative Religion.* Stockholm: Statens Etnografiska Museet.

1979   "Ritual in Native North American Religions." *Native Religious Traditions.* Edited by Earle H. Waugh and K. Dad Prithipaul. Waterloo, Ont.: Wilfrid Laurier Press.

1980   "The Problem of Christian Influence on Northern Algonkian Eschatology." *Studies in Religion* 9: 161-184.

1984   "The American Indian Vision Quest: A Transition Ritual or a Device for Spiritual Aid?" In *I Riti Di Passaggio*: 29-43, edited by Ugo Bianchi. Rome: "L'erma" di Bretschneider.

JACOBS, WILBUR R.

1985   *Dispossessing the American Indian.* Norman: University of Oklahoma Press.

JENNINGS, FRANCIS

1976   *The Invasion of America: Indians, Colonialism and the Cant of Conquest.* New York: W. W. Norton.

JOHNSTON, WILLIAM G.

1892   *Experiences of a Forty-niner.* Pittsburgh.

JORGENSON, JOSEPH G.

1972   *The Sun Dance Religion, Power for the Powerless.* Chicago: University of Chicago Press.

KENT, BARRY C.

1984   *Susquehanna's Indians.* Pennsylvania Historical and Museum Commission, Anthroplogical Series 6. Harrisburg.

KENYON, W.A.

1986   *The History of James Bay 1610-1686. Royal Ontario Museum Archeology Monograph* 10.

KESSELL, JOHN L.

1978   "Diego Romero, the Plains Apaches, and the Inquisition." *The American West* 15(3): 12-16.

KING, J.C.H.

1977   *Smoking Pipes of the North American Indian*. London: British Museum Publications.

1982   *Thunderbird and Lightning: Indian Life in Northeastern North America*. London: British Museum Publications.

KINIETZ, W. VERNON

1965   *The Indians of the Western Great Lakes, 1615-1760*. Ann Arbor: University of Michigan Press.

KROEBER, ALFRED L.

1907   "The Arapaho." *Bull. of the American Museum of Natural History* 18.

1907a   "Gros Ventre Myths and Tales." *American Museum of Natural History Anthropological Papers* 1: 55-139.

KURZ, RUDOLPH FRIEDRICH

1937   *Journal of Rudolph Friedrich Kurz*. Translated by Myrtis Jarrell. Edited by J.N.B. Hewitt. *Bureau of American Ethnology, Bull.* 115.

LA BARRE, WESTON

1975   *The Peyote Cult*, 4th edition. New York: Schocken Books.

LA FLESCHE, FRANCIS

n.d.   Correspondence in Peabody Museum of Archaeology and Ethnology archives.

1921   *The Osage Tribe. 36th Annual Report, Bureau of American Ethnology, 1914-1915*.

LAFITAU

1724   *Moeurs des Sauvages Amériquains*. Paris.

LAHONTAN, BARON

1703   *Some New Voyages into North America*. London.

LAME DEER, JOHN (FIRE), AND ERDOES, RICHARD

1972   *Lame Deer: Seeker of Visions*. New York: Simon and Schuster, paperback edition, 1976)

LEACOCK, ELEANOR

1978   "Women's Status in Egalitarian Society: Implications for Social Evolution." *Current Anthropology* 19: 247-275.

LESCARBOT, MARC

1608   *Histoire de la Nouvelle France*. Paris

LEWIS AND CLARK

1814   *Expedition to the Rocky Mountains*. Philadelphia.

LINTON, RALPH

1923   *Purification of the Sacred Bundles, A Ceremony of the Pawnee. Field Museum of Natural History Leaflet* 7.

1924   *Use of Tobacco Among North American Indians. Field Museum Natural History Leaflet* 19.

LONG, J.

1791   *Voyages and Travels of an Indian Interpreter and Trader.* London.

LONG, STEPHEN J.

1823   *Expedition From Pittsburgh to the Rocky Mountains.* Philadelphia.

LOWIE, ROBERT H.

1913   "Societies of the Hidatsa and Mandan Indians." *Anthropological Papers of the American Museum of Natural History* 11(3): 1-105.

1919   "The Tobacco Society of the Crow Indians." *Anthropological Papers of the American Museum of Natural History* 21(2).

1922   "The Material Culture of the Crow Indians." *Anthropological Papers of the American Museum of Natural History* 21(3): 201-270.

1924   "Minor Ceremonies of the Crow Indians." *Anthropological Papers of the American Museum of Natural History* 21(5): 323-365.

1935   *The Crow Indians.* New York: Holt, Rinehart and Winston.

MARGRY, PIERRE

1875   *Découvertes et Etablissements des Francais, Recit de Nicolas de La Salle, 1684.* Paris.

1875a   *Déscosuvertes et Etablissements des Francais, Relation de l'Abbe de Gallinee.* Paris.

MARTIN, PAUL S.

1936   *Lowry Ruins in Southwestern Colorado. Field Museum of Natural History Anthropological Series* 23.

1964   *Chapters in the Prehistory of Eastern Arizona II. Field Museum of Natural History Anthropological Series* 55.

MASON, J. ALDEN

1924   *Use of Tobacco in Mexico and South America.* Field Museum of Natural History Leaflets 16.

MATHEWS, ZENA PEARLSTONE

1976   "Huron Pipes and Iroquoian Shamanism." *Man in the Northeast* 12: 15-31.

1979   "Pipes With Human Figures From Ontario and Western New York." *American Indian Art* 4(Summer): 43-47.

MATTHIESSEN, PETER

1983   *In the Spirit of Crazy Horse.* New York: The Viking Press.

MAXIMILIAN, PRINCE ZU WIED

1839   *Reise in das Innere Nord Amerika.* Coblentz.

McCLINTOCK, WALTER

1910   *The Old North Trail, or Life, Legends and Religion of the Blackfeet Indians.* Reprint. Lincoln: University of Nebraska Press, 1968.

McCRACKEN, HAROLD

1959   *George Catlin and the Old Frontier.* New York: Bonanza.

MCDERMOTT, JOHN FRANCIS

1961   *Seth Eastman, Pictorial Historian of the Indians*. Norman: University of Oklahoma Press.

1967   *Rudolph Friedrich Kurz, A Swiss Artist on the American Frontier. American Scene* 8(3). Tulsa: Gilcrease Institute.

MCGUIRE, JOSEPH D.

1899   "Pipes and Smoking Customs of the American Aborigines, Based on Material in the U.S. National Museum." *Annual Report of the Smithsonian Institution, 1897* I: 351-645.

MCKERN, W. C.

1945   "Preliminary Report on the Upper Mississippi Phase in Wisconsin." *Milwaukee Public Museum Bull*. 16(3): 109-285.

MCTAGGART, FRED

1984   *Wolf That I Am*. Norman: University of Oklahoma Press.

MICHAELSEN, ROBERT S.

1983   " 'We Also Have Religion.' The Free Exercise of Religion Among Native Americans." *American Indian Quarterly* 7(3): 111-142.

MICHELSON, TRUMAN

1921   *The Owl Sacred Pack of the Fox Indians. Bureau of American Ethnology, Bull*. 72.

MONTGOMERY, HENRY

1906   "Remains of Prehistoric Man in the Dakotas." *American Anthropologist* 8: 640-651.

MOONEY, JAMES

1900   "Myths of the Cherokee." *19th Annual Report, Bureau of American Ethnology, 1897-98:* 3-548.

MOOREHEAD, WARREN K.

1922   "The Hopewell Mound Group of Ohio." *Field Museum of Natural History Anthropological Series* 6(5).

MORGAN, LEWIS HENRY

1851   *League of the Ho-de-no-sau-nee, or Iroquois*. Rochester: Sage and Brother.

MORRIS, EDMUND MONTAGUE

1985   *The Diaries of Edmund Montague Morris, Western Journeys 1907-1910*. Transcribed by Mary FitzGibbon. Toronto: Royal Ontario Museum.

MURIE, JAMES R.

1914   "Pawnee Indian Societies." *Anthopological papers of the American Museum of Natural History* 11(7): 543-644.

MURRAY, ROBERT A.

1965   *Pipestone, A History*. Pipestone: Pipestone Indian Shrine Association.

NICOLAS, LOUIS

1664–   *Codex Canadiensis*. Mss. Gilcrease Institute, Tulsa.
1674

PAPER, JORDAN

1978   "The Meaning of the T'ao-t'ieh." *History of Religions 18: 18-41*

1980   "From Shaman to Mystic in Ojibwa Religion." *Studies in Religion* 9: 185-99.

1983   "The Post-contact Origin of an American Indian High God: The Suppression of Feminine Spirituality." *American Indian Quarterly* 7(4): 1-24.

1986   "The *Feng* in Protohistoric Chinese Religion." *History of Religions* 25: 213-35.

1988   "The Ritual Core of Chinese Religion." *Religious Studies and Theology* (in press).

PARK, WILLARD Z.

1934   "Paviotso Shamanism." *American Anthropologist* N.S. 36: 98-113.

PATTERSON, E. PALMER, II

1972   *The Canadian Indian, A History Since 1500.* Toronto: Collier MacMillan Canada.

PENNY, DAVID W.

1985   "The Late Archaic Period." In *Ancient Art of the American Woodland Indians*, edited by Brose, Brown, and Penny. New York: Harry N. Abrams.

PETRONE, PENNY

1983   *First People, First Voices.* Toronto: University of Toronto Press.

PHILLIPS, RUTH B.

1984   *Patterns of Power: The Jasper Grant Collection in the Royal Irish Museum.* Kleinberg, Ontario: McMichael Canadian Collection.

PICKETT, JAMES ALBERT

1851   *A History of Alabama, and Incidentally of Georgia and Mississippi.* Charleston.

POWELL, PETER J.

1969   *Sweet Medicine.* Norman: University of Oklahoma Press.

POWERS, WILLIAM K.

1982   *Yuwipi.* Lincoln: University of Nebraska Press.

RADIN, PAUL

1923   "The Winnebago Tribe." *Bureau of American Ethnology, Smithsonian Institution, 37th Annual Report:* 1-511.

1945   *The Road of Life and Death.* Princeton: Princeton University Press.

ROBICSEK, FRANCIS

1978   *The Smoking Gods, Tobacco in Maya Art, History and Religion.* Norman: University of Oklahoma Press.

ROGERS, ROBERT

1765   *A Concise Account of North America.* London.

RUSSELL, FRANK

1908   "The Pima Indians." *Bureau of American Ethnology, Annual Report* 26: 3-389.

RUTSCH, EDWARD S.

1973   *Smoking Technology of the Aborigines of the Iroquois Area of New York State*. Rutherford, N.J.: Farleigh Dickinson University.

SAUER, CARL O.

1980   *Seventeenth Century North America*. Berkeley: Turtle Island Foundation.

SCHAEFFER, CLAUDE E.

n.d.   Manuscript papers. Glenbow-Alberta Institute Archives. File Folder 133.

SCHERER, JOANNA COHAN

1973   *Indians*. Reprint. New York: Bonanza, 1982.

SCHULTES, RICHARD EVANS

1972   "An Overview of Hallucinogens in the Western Hemisphere." In *Flesh of the Gods: The Ritual Use of Hallucinogens*, edited by Peter T. Furst. New York: Praeger.

SCHULTZ-THULIN, AXEL

1976   *Indianer der Prarien und Plains*. Stuttgart: Linden-Museum.

SIDOFF, PHILLIP G.

1977   "An Ethnohistorical Investigation of the Medicine Bundle Complex Among Selected Tribes of the Great Plains." *The Wisconsin Archaeologist* 58: 173-204.

SIEGEL, R.K., P.R. COLLINGS, AND J.L. DIAZ

1977   "On the Use of *Tages lucinda* and *Nicotiana rustica* as a Huichol Smoking Mixture: The Aztec 'Yahutli' with Suggestive Hallucinogenic Effects." *Economic Botany* 31: 16-23.

SKINNER, ALANSON

1911   "Notes on the Eastern Cree and Northern Salteaux." *Anthropological Papers of the American Museum of Natural History* 9(1): 1-177.

1913   "Social Life and Ceremonial Bundles of the Menomini Indians." *Anthropological Papers of the American Museum of Natural History* 13(1): 1-105.

1914   "Political Organization, Cults and Ceremonies of the Plains Cree." *Anthropological Papers of the American Museum of Natural History* 11(6): 475-542.

1926   "Ethnology of the Ioway Indians." *Bulletin of the Public Museum of Milwaukee* 5: 181-354.

SMITH, DONALD B.

1984   "Historic Peace-Pipe." *The Beaver* Summer: 4-7.

SOLECKI, RALPH S.

1953   *Exploration of the Adena Mound at Natrium, West Virginia*. Bureau of American Ethnology, Bull. 151.

SPECK, FRANK G.

1935   *Naskapi*. Norman: University of Oklahoma Press

SPRINGER, JAMES WARRREN

    1981   "An Ethnohistoric Study of the Smoking Complex in Eastern North America." *Ethnohistory* 28: 217-235.

STABLER, ARTHUR P.

    1986   *André Thevet's North America, A Sixteenth-Century View.* Montreal: McGill-Queen's University Press.

STARKLOFF, CARL

    1974   *The People of the Center, American Indian Religion and Christianity.* New York: The Seabury Press.

STEINMETZ, PAUL B.

    1980   *Pipe, Bible and Peyote Among the Oglala Lakota.* Stockholm Studies in Comparative Religion.

    1984   "The Sacred Pipe in American Indian Religions." *American Indian Culture and Research Journal* 8(3): 27-80.

STEPHEN, ALEXANDER W.

    1936   *Hopi Journal.* 2 vol. *Columbia University Contributions to Anthropology* 23.

STEWART, OMER C.

    1987   *Peyote Religion, A History.* Norman: University of Oklahoma Press.

SWANTON, JOHN R.

    1946   *The Indians of the Southeastern United States. Bureau of American Ethnology, Bull.* 137.

THEVET, ANDRÉ

    1575   *La Cosmographie universelle d'André Thevet, cosmographe du roy.*

THOMAS, SIDNEY J.

    1941   "A Sioux Medicine Bundle." *American Anthropologist* N.S. 43: 605-609.

THOMPSON, JUDY

    1977   *The North American Indian Collection: A Catalogue.* Berne: Historical Museum.

THWAITES, REUBEN G., ED.

    1896–   *The Jesuit Relations and Allied Documents, Travels and Explorations of*
    1901   *the Jesuit Missionaries in New France, 1610-1791.* 73 vols. Cleveland: Burrows Brothers.

    1959   *Original Journals of the Lewis and Clark Expedition, 1804-1806.* New York: Antiquarian Press.

TOOKER, ELIZABETH

    1964   *An Ethnography of the Huron Indians, 1616-49. Bureau of American Ethnology, Bull.* 169.

TRIGGER, BRUCE G.

    1985   *Natives and Newcomers, Canada's "Heroic Age" Reconsidered.* Montreal: McGill-Queen's Press.

TURNBAUGH, WILLIAM

1977   "Elements of Nativistic Pipe Ceremonialism in the Post-Contact Northeast." *Pennsylvania Archaeologist* 47(4): 1-7.

1979   "Calumet Ceremonialism as a Nativistic Response." *American Antiquity* 44: 685-691.

1980   "Cloudblowers and Calumets." In *Fifth Annual Plains Indian Seminar in Honor of Dr. John C. Ewers*, edtied by George P. Horse Capture and Gene Ball. Cody, Wyoming: Buffalo Bill Historical Center.

1984   "The Sacred Pipe in American Indian Religions." *American Indian Culture and Research Journal* 8(3): 27-80.

VECSEY, CHRISTOPHER

1984   "American Indian Spiritual Politics," *Commonweal* 6 April: 203-208.

1987   "Sun Dances, Corn Pollen, & the Cross." *Commonweal* 5 June: 345-351.

VOGET, FRED W.

1984   *The Shoshoni-Crow Sun Dance*. Norman: University of Oklahoma Press.

WALKER, JAMES R.

1917   "The Sun Dance and Other Ceremonies of the Oglala Division of the Teton Dakota." *American Museum of Natural History Anthropological Papers* 16: 51-221.

1980   *Lakota Belief and Ritual*. Raymond J. DeMallie and Elaine A. Jahner, eds. Lincoln: University of Nebraska Press.

WALLACE, ANTHONY F.C.

1966   *Religion, An Anthropological View*. New York: Random House.

1969   *The Death and Rebirth of the Seneca*. New York: Alfred A Knopf.

WALLACE, R.G., AND FORBES, R. BROWN

1963   "Three Micmac Pipes of North Central Saskatchewan." *Plains Anthropologist* 8: 167-170.

WALTHALL, JOHN A.

1980   *Prehistoric Indians of the Southeast*. University, Alabama: University of Alabama Press.

WALUM OLUM OR *RED SCORE*

1954   *The Migration Record of the Lenni Lenape or Delaware Indians*. Indianapolis: Indiana Historical Society.

WATERS, FRANK

1963   *Book of the Hopi*. New York: Viking Press.

WATSON, PAMELA

1983   *The Precious Foliage: A Study of the Aboriginal Psycho-active Drug Pituri*. Sydney: University of Sydney Press.

WEDEL, MILDRED SCOTT

1959   *Oneota Sites on the Upper Iowa River. The Missouri Archaeologist* 21(2-4).

WEST, GEORGE A.

1934   *Tobacco, Pipes and Smoking Customs of the American Indians. Bulletin of the Public Museum of the City of Milwaukee* 17: 1-994.

WILBERT, JOHANNES

1972   "Tobacco and Shamanistic Ecstasy Among the Warao Indians of Venezuela." In *Flesh of the Gods: The Ritual use of Hallucinogens*, edited by Peter T. Furst. New York: Praeger.

1987   *Tobacco and Shamanism in South America.* New Haven: Yale University Press.

WILDSCHUT, WILLIAM

1975   *Crow Indian Medicine Bundles.* New York: Museum of the American Indian.

WILL, GEORGE F., AND HYDE, GEORGE E.

1917   *Corn Among the Indians of the Upper Missouri.* Reprint. Lincoln: University of Nebraska Press, 1964.

WILLIAMS, ROGER

1643   *A Key Into the Language of America.* London.

WILLOUGHBY, CHARLES C.

1935   *Antiquities of the New England Indians.* Cambridge: Harvard University Press.

WILSON, GILBERT LIVINGSTONE

1928   "Hidatsa Eagle Trapping." *American Museum of Natural History Anthropological Papers* 30(4): 99-245.

WISSLER, CLARK

1910   "Material Culture of the Blackfoot Indians." *American Museum of Natural History Anthropological Papers* 5(1): 1-175.

1912   "Ceremonial Bundles of the Blackfoot Indians." *American Museum of Natural History Anthropological Papers* 7(2): 65-298.

1913   "Societies of the Blackfoot Indians." *American Museum of Natural History Anthropological Papers* 11(4): 358-460.

WITTHOFT, JOHN; SCHOFF, HARRY; AND WRAY, CHARLES F.

1953   "Micmac Pipes, Vase-shaped Pipes, and Calumets." *Pennsylvania Archaeologist* 23: 89-107.

Index